MW01056099

EVERGLADES
WONDROUS RIVER OF LIFE

BY STEVEN L. WALKER & MATTI P. MAJORIN

Above: This young Florida panther is among the last of the panther population to be found in the eastern United States. So few of these large cats remain they have been declared an endangered species and given special legal protection.
PHOTO BY JOHN NETHERTON

Front Cover: A Great Egret and a Snowy Egret, members of the heron family, among the shallow waters of the Everglades National Park.
PHOTO BY GLENN VAN NIMWEGEN

Left: The Great Blue Heron reaches heights of 54 inches, with a wingspan of seven feet, and is the largest and most widespread member of the heron family found in North America.
PHOTO BY JEFF FOOTT

Right: An American alligator glides through the slowly moving waters of the Everglades National Park as the last rays of the sun set.
PHOTO BY ART WOLFE

Designed and Published by Camelback Design Group, Inc. and Elan Publishing, Acc. 6625 North Scottsdale Road, Scottsdale, Arizona USA 85250 Telephone: 602-948-4233.

Requests for additional information should be made to: Camelback/Elan Venture at the address above, or call our toll free telephone number: 1-800-284-6539

Library of Congress Catalog Number: 92-070828
International Standard Book Number: 1-879924-05-6

 Proudly Printed and Bound in the U.S.A.

INTRODUCTION

The Everglades has a history of things left undiscovered, and thought without redeeming value, until the brink of extinction threatens and man finally wakes up. The earliest known inhabitants, the Tequesta and Calusa Indians, were completely eradicated, now we marvel at their cultures through studies of the ruins of their civilizations by archaeologists. The great wading birds, once numbering in the millions, were reduced to a fraction of their former populations by the greed of feather merchants whose craving for profits nearly caused mass extinction as they relentlessly raided rookeries and slaughtered birds for a handful of feathers to adorn women's hats. Alligators and crocodiles were nearly hunted out of existence so their hides could be used in luggage, shoes, and handbags. Species by species, the flora and fauna of the Everglades has come to the brink, the Florida panthers and the manatees are there today, and each time a handful of dedicated people fight to bring them back. Today, it is not a handful of individual species that are threatened, it is the entire ecosystem that is now on the line. Saving it will take more than a handful of concerned people, it will take education and cooperation by the media, politicians, and the general public. The good news, with the addition of vital acreage to the park and the current reversal of earlier water management mistakes to the Everglades' ecosystem, its beginning to happen now.

Although Everglades National Park is the best known preserve in Florida and one of the best known National Parks in the United States, it is far from being the only national preserve, or park, on the Florida Peninsula. The state of Florida is home to two National Parks, two National Seashores, three National Forests, and many national wildlife refuges and state parks.

Florida, a 477 mile long peninsula bordered on one side by the Atlantic Ocean and on the other by the Gulf of Mexico, has the longest coastline of any state in the continental U. S., and is home to the second largest body of freshwater found in the country. These sea and freshwater systems are two of the most important ingredients in creating the unique environments found on the Florida Peninsula. Warm water currents bordering the coastlines bring subtropical weather to the area, and the freshwater present in more than 30,000 lakes and other bodies of water, form an intricate interconnected ecological system throughout southern regions of the state, giving birth to a mixture of tropical and temperate plants and animals unique in all of North America.

In this unique environment the Everglades were formed. Named "Pa-Hay-Okee", or grassy waters by its early Indian inhabitants, later popularized as the "River of Grass", by famous author Marjorie Stoneman Douglas in her 1947 book of the same name, the Everglades are part of a large interconnected ecosystem through which lakes, streams, sloughs, and wetlands extend from the north of Lake Okeechobee to Orlando and above, and south to Florida Bay and the Gulf of Mexico. The Everglades are in fact a long shallow river, up to 50 miles wide and more than 100 miles long, which originally flowed unobstructed from Lake Okeechobee to waters of Florida Bay. Because the peninsula is extremely flat, with a slope of only two to three inches per mile, waters of the Everglades appear to barely flow as they move southward.

The heart of the Everglades system is the wet season and waters of Lake Okeechobee, the blood is the freshwater which has been flowing southwest on the Florida Peninsula for millenniums. This massive ecosystem is the habitat for countless species of plants and animals. Currently, more than 1,000 species of seed bearing plants are known to exist in the Everglades, along with some 120 species of trees, and countless shrubs, vines, and more primitive species of ferns, mosses, and lichens. All of which depend on the life blood of the Everglades, the unobstructed flow of water.

Everglades National Park is home to more than 40 species of mammals, including white tailed deer, black bear, and the endangered Florida Panther; 3 species of aquatic mammals including the endangered West Indian manatee; more than 350 different bird species including some of the rarest and most beautiful species found in the U.S.; and more than fifty species of reptiles including alligators and crocodiles.

Unwise water management policies in the last century have drastically altered the flow of the Everglades, as water was diverted for growing populations and agricultural projects. Natural balance of the Everglades has been upset, with results that threaten the entire ecosystem.

Preceding Pages: Palmetto and cattails under the clear skies of Everglades National Park.
PHOTO BY DAVID MUENCH

Left: Reddish Egrets are active feeders in shallow waters employing a special technique known as canopy feeding. The Reddish Egret forages with its wings spread over the water, creating pools of shadow, through which it can better see its prey.
PHOTO BY ART WOLFE

Right: Mangrove at Florida Bay. For many years mangroves were removed to make room for more and more land development. Today, we know that the mangroves are instrumental in the formation of additional landmass and in protection of coastal areas from the ravages of weather and tides.
PHOTO BY DAVID MUENCH

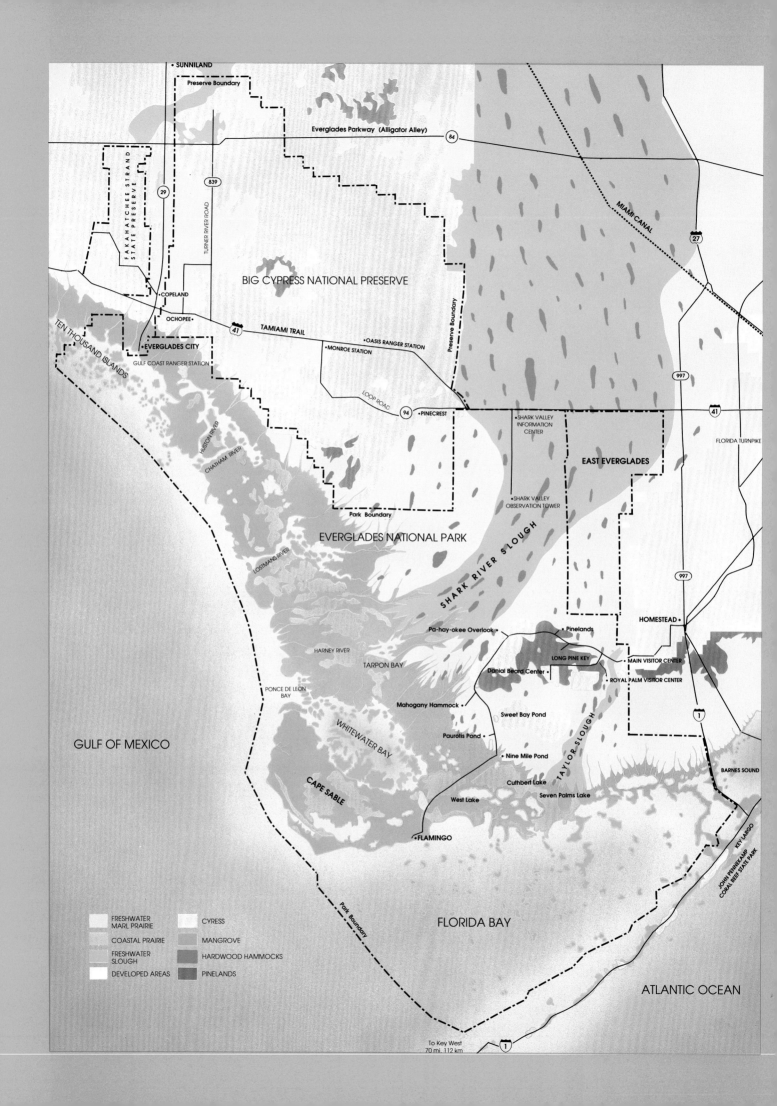

• SUNNILAND

Preserve Boundary

Everglades Parkway (Alligator Alley) 84

MIAMI CANAL

29

839

27

FAKAHATCHEE STRAND STATE PRESERVE

TURNER RIVER ROAD

BIG CYPRESS NATIONAL PRESERVE

• COPELAND

OCHOPEE •

41 TAMIAMI TRAIL

• OASIS RANGER STATION

Preserve Boundary

997

• EVERGLADES CITY

• MONROE STATION

Gulf Coast Ranger Station

41

TEN THOUSAND ISLANDS

LOOP ROAD

94 • PINECREST

FLORIDA TURNPIKE

HUSTON RIVER

CHATHAM RIVER

• SHARK VALLEY INFORMATION CENTER

EAST EVERGLADES

• SHARK VALLEY OBSERVATION TOWER

Park Boundary

EVERGLADES NATIONAL PARK

SHARK RIVER SLOUGH

LOSTMANS RIVER

997

Pa-hay-okee Overlook • • Pinelands

HOMESTEAD •

HARNEY RIVER

Danial Beard Center •

LONG PINE KEY

MAIN VISITOR CENTER

TARPON BAY

• ROYAL PALM VISITOR CENTER

Mahogany Hammock •

PONCE DE LEON BAY

Sweet Bay Pond

1

WHITEWATER BAY

Paurotis Pond •

TAYLOR SLOUGH

GULF OF MEXICO

• Nine Mile Pond

BARNES SOUND

CAPE SABLE

Cuthbert Lake

West Lake

Seven Palms Lake

KEY LARGO

• FLAMINGO

JOHN PENNEKAMP CORAL REEF STATE PARK

Park Boundary

FLORIDA BAY

ATLANTIC OCEAN

FRESHWATER MARL PRAIRIE   CYRESS

COASTAL PRAIRIE   MANGROVE

FRESHWATER SLOUGH   HARDWOOD HAMMOCKS

DEVELOPED AREAS   PINELANDS

To Key West
70 mi, 112 km   1

GEOGRAPHY

Everglades National Park, located at the southern tip of the Florida Peninsula, is the largest subtropical wilderness remaining in the United States. The region consists of extensive fresh and saltwater areas, open prairies, and mangrove forests. Here, temperate zones meet with the subtropics, featuring a blend of the flora and fauna of both, in habitats totally unique to the region.

Everglades National Park has many distinct environments: the saltwater keys of Florida Bay; the coastal prairie; mangrove forests in brackish swamps; cypress swamps; vast freshwater marshes with tree islands and ponds which are the true Everglades; and the pine and hammock rocklands, which is the driest zone in the region. Each of these habitats play an important role in the continuation of the entire Everglades system.

The Everglades extend far beyond the borders of Everglades National Park and includes the Big Cypress National Preserve on its northern boundaries, they extend even further, to the north of Lake Okeechobee; east to the Atlantic coast; and flow south to enter the salty waters of Florida Bay and the Gulf of Mexico. The Everglades National Park, (See map opposite page), alone covers an area of 2,354 square miles, or 1,506,539 acres, which is only a fraction of the Everglades' total land area.

The Everglades offer a scenic beauty that may escape many visitors at first glance. The entire region is extremely flat, there are no majestic mountains or giant chasms here, and reaches altitudes that are no more than ten feet above sea level. Often, the horizon blends with the waters of the region and are devoid of dramatic punctuations. The scenic beauty and natural wonder of the Everglades requires closer inspection, into the cycles of life found within its confines, and rewards those taking the time and effort to observe habitats and animal species that exist in few other places.

A large system of interconnected rivers, streams, lakes, and wetland swamps feeds the Everglades region from as far to the north as Orlando, Florida. The Everglades is actually a huge hydrologic system covering the entire southern half of the state of Florida. The slowly flowing waters of the Everglades ensure the survival and delicate balance of the entire region's ecosystems.

Unlike the rest of the continental United States, the Everglades experiences only two seasons, dry and wet, or winter and summer. Winter is the dry season and brings cool, comfortable temperatures from November to the end of April each year, with frost a rarity. The winter season also brings droughts to the region. Although the term drought often brings negative connotations of parched surroundings to most people's minds, they are necessary in the continuing cycle of life for the area.

The wet, or summer season, falls between the months of May and October and accounts for nearly 80 percent of the region's annual rainfall. During this season, thunderstorms, lightning, and heavy rains are the norm, with occasional hurricanes a possibility any time between June and November. During the wet summer season, lightning strikes the south of Florida with more frequency than in any

Everglades National Park in south Florida contains more than 1,500,000 acres of sawgrass prairies, hammocks, and mangrove swamps and is the site of the world's largest freshwater marsh. Earliest references to the Everglades appeared on English maps made during the eighteenth century when surveyor Gerard de Brahm mapped the area and identified the Everglades as "River Glades," which was used to denote the presence of the river and the glades, a term used to describe open spaces surrounded by woods. Later maps by the English found the word "River" changed to "Ever" and in 1823 a map denoting the area as the "Everglades" was first published, coining a name for the river of grass that was used thereafter.

Preceding Pages: Mangrove trees at sunrise. The mangroves play an important role in protecting shorelines from the ravages of storms and from encroaching seas while adding new landmass as peats and soils accumulate around their roots.
PHOTO BY CARR CLIFTON

Right: The region's Indians called the Everglades "Pa-hay-okee," which means "grassy water." The slow moving shallow waters of the Everglades are part of a gigantic wetlands system that originates near Orlando, in the center of Florida, and flows to the state's southernmost bays.
PHOTO BY MARK MUENCH

other location in the Continental United States. These summer rains are necessary for the survival and sustenance of the Everglades, renewing the supply of fresh water during the repeating cycle of drought and flood. With an annual mean rainfall of approximately 53 inches, the Everglades still experiences great variations in rainfall from one year to the next, with wetter years peaking at close to one hundred inches and in years experiencing severe droughts far less rain falls than the norm, with as few as thirty inches recorded.

The Everglades ecosystem has a subtropical climate very similar to that of the Caribbean. The Gulf Stream flows warm water currents along the eastern coastline of Florida and the prevailing easterly and southeasterly winds carry their warm tropical air inland toward the Everglades. The influence of the tropical air currents, and temperate air currents of the Continental United States, create combinations of tropical and temperate flora that are unique in all the world. Temperate plants, such as

willows, poison ivy, and Virginia creeper, have migrated down the Florida Peninsula from the north to combine with cocoplum,

The state of Florida is the southernmost land mass in the continental United States. Florida was discovered by Juan Ponce de Leon on Easter Sunday of 1513. De Leon claimed the area for the Spanish king and named it Florida, meaning "feast of flowers."

strangler fig, and gumbo limbo, which are tropical species that had originally arrived in

the Everglades region, borne on the wind and water, or deposited by birds visiting the area from the islands of the West Indies.

During the wet season, hurricanes frequent south Florida. More hurricanes have ripped through Florida than in any other area of the United States. During this century, more than fifty hurricanes have attacked Florida, violently ripping trees and plants from the ground. In September of 1960, Hurricane Donna ravaged south Florida and destroyed much of the mature mangrove forests along the Gulf Coast.

With winds that exceed 75 miles per hour, and can approach 200 miles per hour, at first glance hurricanes appear to only deliver mass destruction. In fact, the fierce winds and heavy rains accompanying hurricanes open new places for renewed plant growth, spread seed far and wide, and thoroughly mix the shallow waters of the region to change the nutrient supplies for the higher levels of the food chain.

Winter low temperatures average between 60 degrees and the upper 70's, with the effect

The Influence of the West Indies...

The Florida peninsula has a strong tropical, or as often argued, sub-tropical, influence that is caused in part by warm water and air currents of the Gulf Stream, which brings moist tropical weather to the region, and its location. The tip of the Florida Keys are only 75 miles north of the Tropic of Cancer, but north of the tropical zone nonetheless, which causes a constant source of debate in terms of accurately describing the south Florida region. By scientific definition, tropical zones are not subjected to frosts, which although infrequent, can occur in the Everglades when northern cold fronts hit and will damage crops and the more fragile plant species from the West Indies.

Although the Florida peninsula, located between mainland USA and the West Indies, may not truly qualify as a tropical area, the influence of the West Indies on the flora and fauna of the area makes the entire region at the very least appear tropical. The warm Gulf Stream currents, and often strong carrying winds, including hurricanes, from the West Indies have brought varied species to the south Florida shores and the Everglades. This, coupled with accessible land access for plant and animal species migrating from temperate zones in North America, has enabled the region to attract a unique mixture of plants and animals.

Unfortunately, the areas off of Florida's coast are constantly under stress from pollutants and environmental damages caused by the continual encroachment of land developers in the region. In recent years, the area's coral reefs have also experienced increasing pressure from souvenir hunters who break off pieces of the coral reef, not realizing they are killing living organisms that have taken many years to develop.

In the fragile ecosystem off Florida's coast, the same forces of nature that allowed the tropical species from the West Indies to migrate to south Florida can also play a serious roll. Hurricanes, and strong waves they create, often devastate coastlines and coral reefs.

FLORIDA

GULF OF MEXICO

STRAITS OF FLORIDA

BAHAMAS

ATLANTIC OCEAN

CUBA

MEXICO

WINDWARD PASSAGE

HAITI DOMINICAN REPUBLIC

PUERTO RICO

CARIBBEAN SEA

JAMAICA

JAMAICA CHANNEL

of dramatically reducing mosquitoes to a level bearable to humans. Colder and drier weather also reduces water levels and concentrates bird and animal populations near water holes to add to the scenic enjoyment of visitors.

Summer season, with average temperatures nearing the 90 degree mark with high levels of humidity, raises mosquito and deer fly populations to levels that can become a major nuisance for most visitors. Although biting insects, humidity, and heat can make it difficult to enjoy the Everglades in summer, irritations they may cause can be worth the rewards of experiencing the natural splendor of the region during its most active season.

THE ROLE OF THE MANGROVES...

The role played by the mangroves in the vast ecosystems of the Everglades is many faceted. The mangroves serve as a natural hatchery and nursery for countless species of crustaceans and invertebrates, therefore providing an open food reserve to the higher levels of the food chain as birds, fishes, and other species use the smaller crustaceans and invertebrates readily found in the mangroves as an important source of food. Water currents and tides will carry some of these smaller nutrients away from the coastline, feeding schools of fish and crustaceans found further at sea and along offshore coral reefs.

The mangrove forests play an equally important role in protecting the southern Florida coastline from the devastating effects of bad weather, hurricanes, and the encroaching sea, while at the same time adding to the area's land mass. By their proliferous growth, mangroves create a buffer zone between high winds and waters and the fragile deposits of soils and peats which collect around their roots, and serve to expand the coastline by their growth patterns.

The process of land growth by mangrove trees is an intricate one. As sea currents deposit grains of quartz sand, forming sand bars in the deeper water away from the existing shoreline, oyster beds form and with additional sediments, add to the overall mass of the sand bar. Eventually, these deposits reach a height that leaves them exposed during periods of low tides. As this new base is formed, a fertile growing ground is created for the mangrove trees, which have an ingenious way of spreading their seeds. Mangrove seeds grow, and germinate, while still on the parent tree. The seeds, able to resist salt water and the elements with their protective outer shell, are able to travel long distances on water currents until finding ground favorable for growth.

Mangrove seeds, transported by water currents, then establish themselves and begin to grow on the now exposed sand bar. Once they are firmly established, they supercede the oyster beds and sand deposits and outgrow them in all directions. Forming island after island, the trees often join to form the larger masses of mangroves that are evident throughout the region. It was in this manner the Ten Thousand Islands archipelago was formed. As the mangrove trees live and die, with their leaves and branches rotting in the water, large amounts of peat are deposited, thus forming additional land mass.

Mangrove trees have played an important role in creating the present shoreline of southern Florida, advancing progressively further into bays and ocean waters. Growth for these sturdy trees is hampered, and sometimes destroyed, by hurricanes attacking the Everglades region. The dominant mangrove, the red mangrove, is the only true mangrove and is the most abundantly found in the area. The other salt tolerant trees, the white and black mangroves, along with the buttonwood, are not true mangrove trees but are referred to as mangroves nevertheless. The mangroves grow on the edge of the coastline, expanding its growth in the intertidal zones, while buttonwoods spread further inland and are often found growing within the confines of mahogany hammocks and other hardwood hammocks.

Below: Bacteria and fungi begin the process of breaking down fallen leaves and branches. Crustaceans and other invertebrates further the process and contribute proteins to feed the larger species of fish and mammals.

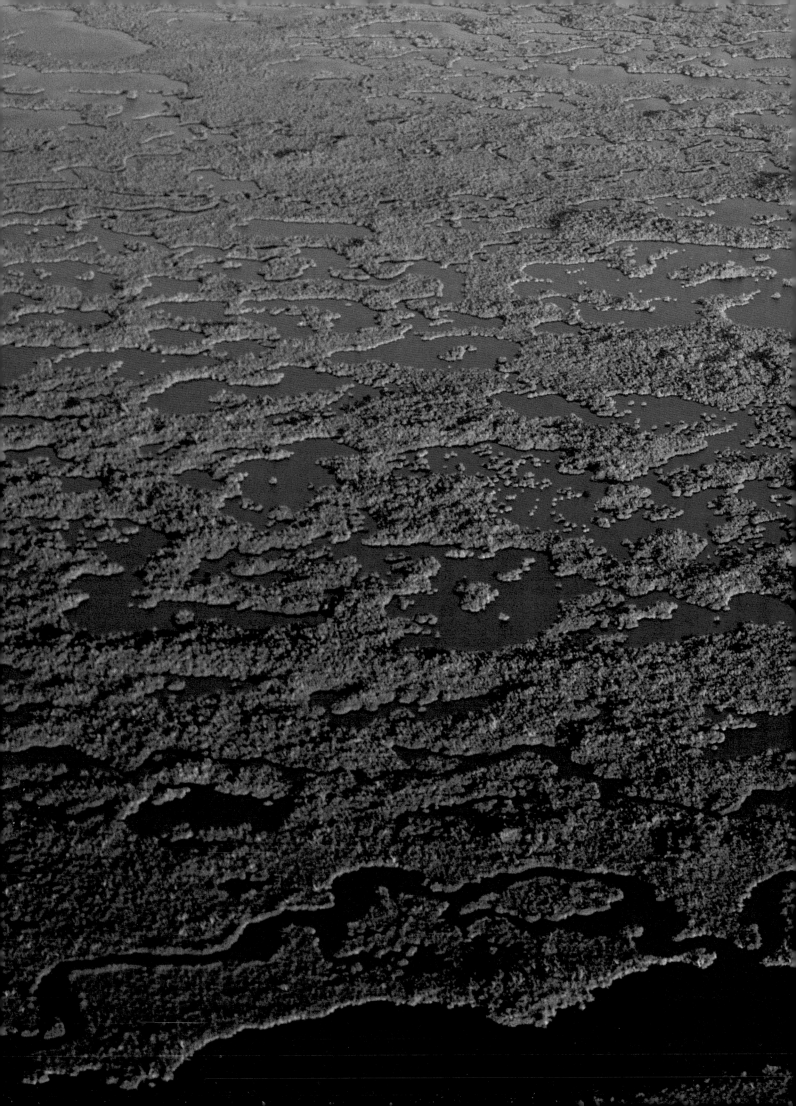

GEOLOGY

South florida is relatively young when compared to most of Earth's land masses, its deepest and oldest deposits, Tamiami limestone, are only around six million years old. Formed between North America, the Gulf of Mexico, and the Atlantic Ocean, the south Florida peninsula has a bedrock base made of volcanic and metamorphic rock materials, covered with thick layers of sedimentary deposits. Since formation, it has been extremely stable and has been without chaotic geological pressures, volcanic activity, and cataclysmic plate tectonic forces found in most regions.

For millions of years, sedimentary deposits settled on the bedrock base at the bottom of seas that periodically covered Florida. As the seas retreated, these deposits were subjected to erosion, partially removing and carving them. This process was repeated time and again until deposits of sediments formed layers up to three miles thick on the bedrock base.

In the last few million years, the Everglades were repeatedly inundated by shallow ocean waters, which then receded and left the land exposed to the elements, a process that was repeated five times during glaciation periods of the Pleistocene Era. These periodic changes in water levels were due mainly to expansion and contraction of the polar ice caps. In glacial times, much of the earth's water was stored in the ice caps and the ocean levels dropped, leaving land exposed. Interglacial periods then raised water levels and the area was flooded.

Scientists believe the ocean is again rising, and argue that sea levels have risen an inch or more per century for the last 14,000 years.

Recent warming of the atmosphere, caused by burning fuel oils and use of chemicals depleting the atmosphere, could accelerate melting of the polar ice caps, causing dramatic consequences for Florida and the Everglades. Small variations in sea levels can produce dramatic changes in the Everglades, which depends highly on the quality of its freshwater supply for survival of much of its flora and fauna.

Although south Florida is extremely flat, with small variations in altitude, its profile is slightly elevated along both coastlines. In the east, relief is created by an eroded outcropping of Miami limestone, which is tilted to the west toward Everglades National Park. On the west coast, more elevated lands create the other side of a shallow basin, through which the waters of the Everglades gently flow. The South Florida Plateau, tilted southwest at a grade of only a few inches per mile, allows the waters of the Everglades to flow to the Gulf of Mexico.

The Everglades rests on a layer of Miami limestone, formed as small particles, called ooids, were deposited in shallow seas. Deeper holes of water collected colonies of marine invertebrates, called bryozoans, who added their shells to the limestone deposits. Beneath the Miami and Fort Thompson formations, a limestone surfacing north of the Park, lies the older and harder Tamiami formation, which contains quartz sand deposits. This formation, less permeable than surface limestone deposits, collects fresh waters seeping from above to form a gigantic freshwater reserve. This huge aquifer serves as a very important source of freshwater reserves for south Florida.

Mangroves play a varied role in the ecosystems of the Everglades, protecting the coastline from the devastating effects of severe storms and the encroaching sea, while adding to the area's land mass by collecting fragile deposits of peats and soils around their roots. The mangroves act as a natural hatchery and nursery for countless species of invertebrates and crustaceans, providing an open food reserve to the higher levels of the food chain as fishes, birds, and other species use the smaller crustaceans and invertebrates found in the mangroves as an important source of food.

Preceding Pages: Waterways wind through islands of vegetation in this aerial view of the Everglades.
PHOTO BY TOM TILL

Left: A great white heron fishing in the shallow waters of Florida Bay near Flamingo. Bryozoan colonies, similar to those which formed much of the dominant constituent of Miami limestone in the park, are still found in Florida Bay.
PHOTO BY LARRY ULRICH

Right: Detail of a beach of shells at Cape Sable on the western edge of Florida Bay.
PHOTO BY TOM TILL

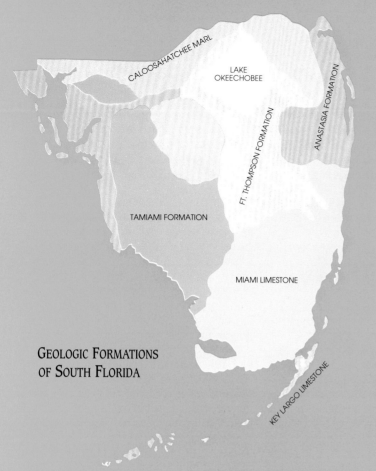

GEOLOGIC FORMATIONS
OF SOUTH FLORIDA

GEOLOGIC TIMETABLE

FORMATION	THICKNESS FEET.	CHARACTERISTICS	AGE	ERA	PERIODS	EPOCHS
MIAMI LIMESTONE	0 - 40'	WHITE TO YELLOWISH COLOR. OOLITIC AND BRYOZOAN FACIES.	100,000			
ANASTASIA FORMATION	0 - 120'	COQUINA, SAND, SHELL MARL, AND CALCAREOUS SANDSTONE	100,000+			HOLOCENE / PLEISTOCENE
KEY LARGO LIMESTONE	0 - 200'	EXCELLENT AQUIFER OF CORALLINE REEF ROCK. HARD AND CAVERNOUS	100,000+	CENOZOIC	QUARTERNARY	
FT. THOMPSON FORMATION	0 - 150'	LIMESTONE, SANDSTONE, ALTERNATING MARINE OR FRESHWATER MARLS	100,000+			
CALOOSA-HATCHEE MARL	0 - 25'	CLAY, SILT, SAND, SHELL BEDS, AND SANDY MARL POOR TO FAIR AQUIFER	2,000,000+			PLIOCENE / MIOCENE
TAMIAMI FORMATION	0 - 100'	HARDENED LIMESTONE OF CLAYEY MARL, SILT, SHELL SAND, SAND MARL	6,000,000		TERTIARY	
UNDERLYING DEPOSITS	UP TO 3 MILES	BEDROCK OF VOLCANIC AND METAMORPHIC ROCK MATERIALS	6,000,000+	MESOZOIC	CRETACEOUS	*

* OLIGOCENE / EOCENE / PALEOCENE

OOIDS AND BRYOZOANS...

The Everglades are situated on several layers of limestone, the most recently deposited being the Miami limestone, which was formed around 100,000 years ago when the area was covered by warm shallow sea waters. The process forming the Miami limestone is by no means a prehistoric process, and continues even today to form new land areas, such as the Bahama Bank across the straits of Florida.

Concentrated by the water currents of the Gulf Stream, small grains and particles called Ooids are deposited to form layers in warm shallow seas containing high levels of calcium carbonate. In deeper holes of water, colonies of bryozoans, small marine invertebrates secreting calcareous shells can be found. The Miami limestone formation includes the remains of billions of bryozoans. The multi-laminate bryozoans,

Schizoporella floridana, were largely responsible for Miami limestone formations beneath the Park, comprising up to 70 percent of the mass in places.

Beneath Lake Okeechobee, rocky formations begin that continue under the Everglades. These limestone deposits are of harder rock containing muds and peats. Continuing to the south, the limestone deposits, called Oolite, are more porous and contain shells, sand, and decomposing flora to form receptacles for fresh water.

Underneath the Big Cypress National Preserve northwest of the Everglades, and sloping beneath the Miami and Fort Thompson formations, is the much older Tamiami formation. More than six million years old, the Tamiami formation contains much harder deposits of quartz sand and is less permeable than the layers of limestone found above, forming a freshwater aquifer.

OOIDS

BRYOZOANS

WEST

SIERRA NEVADA

ROCKY MOUNTAINS

15,000
12,000
9,000
6,000
3,000
0

South Florida was created by a slow and gentle process that did not include the cataclysmic and chaotic events instrumental in the formation of the mountains and canyons of other regions. The sea deposited sediments on the bedrock base that gradually were compacted and shaped as the land was submerged. As the sea retreated, land was exposed and subjected to erosion.

The basis of the Floridian Plateau, reaching up to 300 miles in width, was created by altered volcanic rock and covered by sedimentary deposits reaching 3 miles thick.

As water levels receded during periods of glaciation, erosion cut valleys and slight areas of relief in the otherwise flat sedimentary layers of deposits in the region.

Water released during periods of interglaciation, covered the region, compacted earlier deposits, and created new layers of sedimentary deposits eliminating relief.

Around 100,000 years ago, during an interglaciation period, limestone deposits were laid containing small grains of sand, called Ooids, and invertebrates called bryozoans.

As water levels again receded, the limestone deposits were eroded, and solidified, into rock. The ooids formed the Atlantic coastal ridge, bryozoans the Everglades base.

As the glaciers melted a final time during the Pleistocene epoch, the region was submerged once again and covered by warm shallow seas that were at least 25 feet deep.

As the cycle completed itself for a final time, sea levels receded and south Florida was shaped into a saucer-like peninsula that carries water for the Everglades.

THE BISCAYNE AQUIFER...

An aquifer is a geologic formation, or geologic formations, containing enough saturated and permeable materials to yield sufficient quantities of water for wells and springs, and are formed as water seeping through porous ground is accumulated above impermeable formations. In south Florida, the lower layers of the Tamiami formation form a base for the Biscayne Aquifer, which provides the largest supply of freshwater for the region.

Fort Thompson and Miami limestone formations are also part of the aquifer. Because of the high level of permeability of these layers, the Biscayne Aquifer is considered one of the most permeable aquifers in the world, easily able to replenish itself during the wet season, and able to capture large amounts of seasonal rains. The availability of water is so great in certain areas that some wellfields can generate up to two thousand gallons of fresh water a minute.

The Biscayne Aquifer was historically able to maintain a natural balance between freshwater and the salty, or brackish, waters of Florida Bay and the ocean. Recently, extreme water usage for agricultural, industrial, and residential purposes, as well as the more rapid flow of water caused by channelization of the Everglades, has reduced the amount of water filtering and seeping through the layers of the aquifer. This abuse has also damaged the ability of the aquifer to maintain the pressures needed to keep salt waters from encroaching into freshwater supplies. Many wells which formerly generated freshwater now produce brackish or salty waters unfit for consumption. Dams and canals have recently been constructed to maintain higher water levels and the necessary pressure to keep the salt water at bay. Reversal of earlier water management mistakes is underway in an effort to save the aquifer.

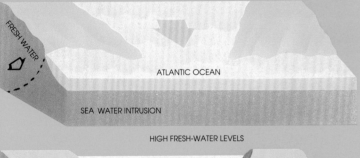

FRESH WATER

ATLANTIC OCEAN

SEA WATER INTRUSION

HIGH FRESH-WATER LEVELS

FRESH WATER

ATLANTIC OCEAN

SEA WATER INTRUSION

LOW FRESH-WATER LEVELS

CROSS SECTION OF SOUTH FLORIDA

OOLITIC FACIES

BRYOZOAN FACIES

ATLANTIC OCEAN

GULF OF MEXICO

ATLANTIC COASTAL RIDGE

UNITED STATES PROFILE

AT PLAINS

CENTRAL LOWLAND

APPALACHIAN HIGHLANDS

COASTAL PLAINS

EAST 20 FEET

LANDSCAPE

The Everglades National Park preserves unique habitats not found elsewhere on the north American continent. The main vegetative zones found in the Everglades region include plant and animal species from both the West Indies and North America. The further south one travels down the Florida Peninsula, the more tropical plant species become, while traveling to the north, species become increasingly more temperate.

The life-blood of the Everglades ecosystems is the rainwater poured on south Florida during the wet summer season. Collected by a vast hydrological network extending as far north as Orlando, and winding its way through Lake Okeechobee, fresh water finally feeds the Everglades from what was once a huge undisturbed river more than one hundred miles long and fifty miles wide, and finally flows into Florida Bay and the Gulf of Mexico.

Everglades National Park contains nearly 485,000 acres of Florida Bay and the Gulf of Mexico. A shallow saltwater bay at the south end of the Florida Peninsula, Florida Bay has little circulation, and is cut off from the ocean by sandbars, dense mangrove growths, and the Florida Keys. The bay is around nine feet at its deepest, and averages between four and five feet deep over much of its area. Estuarine zones, where saltwater and freshwater meet, and marine zones, serve as breeding and spawning grounds for crustaceans, fish, and countless other species necessary as a part of the food chain of the Everglades.

Mangrove forests, which grow in marine and estuarine zones favoring brackish water, perform an important role in the geology of the Everglades as they extend land along the coast and protect the Everglades' interior from erosion by storms. The mangroves seen today are mostly younger trees, as much of the older mangrove growth along the entire Gulf Coast of the park was removed by 180 mph winds of Hurricane Donna in 1960. Prior to Hurricane Donna, mangrove forests of the Everglades were among the world's largest.

Mangrove forests contain areas of coastal prairie in which salt-tolerant plants, including yucca and cactus, are found among grasses. Occasionally, hardwood trees attempt to take root in the thin salty soils or on shell mounds left by prehistoric Indians. The shell mounds, evidence that the Indians used shellfish for food, cover about 135 acres at Chokoloskee near Everglades City, the largest shell mounds still existing. Chokoloskee, with mounds reaching elevations of twenty feet, is the highest point in the Everglades National Park.

Sawgrass Everglades, the largest sawgrass marsh in the world, are also referred to as freshwater marl prairies or freshwater sloughs. These freshwater marshes, dotted with islands of trees called hammocks and heads, cover most of the interior of Everglades National Park. Shark River and Taylor Sloughs are the main channels moving fresh water through the park. Shark River Slough, the larger and more central of the two, is as much as forty miles wide during the wet summer season, although it dwindles into small streams during winter.

The freshwater marl prairies are home to many of the more than 100 species of grasses

Fire plays an important role in the continuing cycle of life in the Everglades. Prior to the arrival of man in the Everglades, periodic fires burned that actually benefited plant and animal species of the region by removing plants that were unable to survive fire damage and allowing new growth. Marsh rabbit, white-tailed deer, and other animal species ate the tender shoots of emerging plants and birds were attracted to burnt areas as certain types of food were more easily found there.

Historically, sawgrass Everglades were seldom damaged since they were the recipients of a water supply that had not yet been constricted by man's water management policies. Slash pine and saw palmetto, relying on fires to remove hardwoods and other plants that establish themselves in the pinelands, have thick barks to protect them from fire, and their seedlings grow best in soils mixed with ash and removed of competing vegetation.

After man's arrival, fires were controlled until it became evident they played important roles in the ecosystem's balance. Today, fires deliberately set and controlled are part of the park's management.

Left: Coastal prairie near Eco Pond in Everglades National Park. The coastal prairies feature low ground covering plants that are able to tolerate occasional intrusions of salt water to take root among grasses growing in the thin salty soils.
PHOTO BY LARRY ULRICH

Right: Snowy egrets fishing among the arched roots of a red mangrove. Favoring the brackish waters of marine and estuarine zones, mangrove forests add new land to the region by extending their seeds into waters offshore and capturing sediments among their roots.
PHOTO BY JEFF FOOTT

found in the Everglades, and include deeper ponds and gator holes necessary for survival of the regions species during winter months. The sawgrass of the Everglades is not a grass but is actually a sedge, a grasslike marsh plant with three sharp toothed edges and a solid stem, that grows to heights of twelve feet.

Vast expanses of the Everglades are broken by clumps of vegetation, which often take the shape of islands, surrounded by a sea of grass. The origins of these tree islands, also called hammocks and heads, are thought to vary. Some islands were created as higher limestone outcroppings protected seedlings from summer floods, others were created by accumulations of peat and soil that strengthened and expanded to harbor different tree species. Depending upon the species dominating an island, they are named accordingly. Cypress hammocks, or cypress heads, are dominated by cypress trees, bayheads by bay trees, mahogany hammocks have mahogany trees, although they can also often be referred to as hardwood hammocks.

Hammock characters and populations vary throughout the park due to slight variations in altitude, the effects of water levels, seasonal flooding, warming effects of the sea and gulf stream, and their natural abilities to survive wildfires. They are usually made of a variety of mature hardwoods, a large proportion of broad leafed trees, and shrubs native to the southeast United States and the West Indies. West Indian plants are transplanted naturally as their seeds are transported by Gulf Stream currents, borne by winds, or deposited by migratory birds.

Hammocks vary by their positions within the region, those along the Keys and south Florida coast being similar to vegetative types found in Cuba or the Bahamas. Inland, species of northern trees make appearances in hammocks since these areas are not as influenced by warmer air currents.

Near Paradise Key and Mahogany Hammock, average rainfalls are higher and hammocks are richer and fuller, and are thick with various ferns, mosses, and epiphytic species like bromeliad and orchid. Southwestern areas near Cape Sable have less rainfall, reducing size and density of its hammocks as well as the thickness and variety of its ground cover, than hammocks found in in other areas.

Hammocks vary in size from less than an acre to hundreds of acres. Some have been found to contain more than 70 tree species, creating distinct microcosms with stark contrasts to the surrounding areas. The larger trees form canopies shading an undergrowth of vines and shrubs, creating an excellent environment for insects, frogs, snails, snakes, birds, and larger creatures to make their homes and propagate their individual species.

Bayheads, cypress heads, and willow heads usually have forests tangled with vines and trees, including Bay, Magnolia, and Holly. Normally found on elevations of peat soils, they are populated with fewer species of trees than hammocks. During the dry season, they fall prey to wild fires and can often be totally eradicated by the more severe fires.

In sinkholes, depressions, ponds, and lower sites where more water is present, cypress trees may take over and form a cypress head, called cypress domes because of their shapes. These areas are referred to as domes because the trees grow tallest where water is deepest and the soil richest, usually in the center, and then become progressively smaller as they grow toward outer edges, forming the dome.

Pinelands are found in more elevated areas of south Florida on outcroppings of Miami limestone and are predominately comprised of Florida slash pine. Pinelands grow on fertile soil pockets in the limestone deposits, their roots searching into cracks, crevices, and holes in the rock for the most fertile grounds.

Prior to logging practices of the early 1900's and expansion of human populations, forest covered the limestone outcroppings of the Atlantic Coastal Ridge, often four to five miles wide and nearly 50 miles long. The pinelands grew from the north of Fort Lauderdale to the eastern coastal ridge of the Everglades. Today, remains of this vast forest are limited to the confines of Everglades National Park.

Fire plays an important role in limiting the ground cover and hardwoods that compete with slash pine and saw palmetto, including wild poinsettia, pine pink orchids, passion flower, iris, Florida fiddlewood, various shrubs, and hardwoods, and establish themselves in the pinelands. Slash pine and saw palmetto are able to resist devastation caused by fires by limiting damage to the outer layers of their thick bark, protecting their inner tissues from the flames. Recently deposited ashes from fires even aids seedling growth by enriching soils.

Above: This mahogany hammock in Everglades National Park forms an impenetrable thicket.
PHOTO BY JERRY SIEVE

Left: Typical of most Dwarf Cypress ponds, larger trees grow in the center and trees grow smaller toward the outer perimeters, forming a dome.
PHOTO BY DAVID MUENCH

Right: Saw-palmetto forms a solid ground cover amid Florida slash pines in the pinelands.
PHOTO BY LARRY ULRICH

BIG CYPRESS

Prior to the completion of the Tamiami Trail in 1928, the Big Cypress region had giant cypress trees that often grew to heights of 100 to 120 feet and more. The completion of the trail made the area easily accessible and commercial exploitation began as lumbering boomed during the 1930's and 1940's. Cypress wood was long valued for its lasting qualities and prized for use in coffins, boat houses, piers, boats and other projects requiring water resistant woodworking. Most of the giant cypress trees, many as much as 600 to 700 years old, were cut to the ground. Today, the few giant cypress trees remaining are protected, and they continue to play important roles in the life cycles of the big cypress swamp, their branches harbor anhingas, ibis, egrets, cormorants, hawks, the endangered wood storks, and many other species.

The southern tip of the Florida Peninsula is dominated by two large ecosystems: the Everglades, covering approximately four million acres, of which nearly 1.5 million acres are a part of Everglades National Park; and Big Cypress Swamp, covering around 1.5 million acres, with 570,000 acres set aside by Congress in 1974 as Big Cypress National Preserve as a natural buffer protecting the Everglades National Park and wetlands located to the west of its borders.

West of the Big Cypress National Preserve, but still within the boundaries of Big Cypress Swamp, lies the Fakahatchee Strand, an area of about 100,000 acres established as a state wildlife preserve, mainly for the protection of endangered Florida Panthers. Further to the northwest is Corkscrew Swamp, consisting of 11,000 acres designated a National Audubon Society Sanctuary, known for its wood stork nesting colony and for the largest stand of bald cypress remaining in Florida.

The Big Cypress National Preserve, a 2,400 square mile area in south central Florida, is extremely flat, with only minor variations in elevation. The land slopes only two inches per mile toward the Gulf of Mexico and includes vast expanses of saw grass, water (most of the year except during the dry winter season), and unique ecosystems enhanced by large numbers of fish, birds, and mysterious plants, such as epiphytic plants and orchids.

The name Big Cypress Swamp creates vivid images of giant cypress trees amid virtually impenetrable snake and alligator infested swamps, although the name is a misnomer

since the area is actually comprised of a diverse variety of environments: marshes, wet prairies, dry prairies, sandy islands of slash pine, the mixed hardwood hammocks, and coastal mangrove forests.

The Big Cypress region is covered on only about one-third of its area by cypress trees, and these are not the large cypress trees that existed prior to the 1930's, but are mostly the dwarf cypress variety, trees that are often a more than a hundred years old but remain small because of particularly poor growing conditions. The wide expanse of dwarf cypress trees, often called the dwarf Cypress savannah, has trees dwarfed to heights of only a few feet, often mistaken for seedlings.

Cypress growth occurs in two major forms: one covering large areas with great numbers of trees similar in size; while the other is found in dome shaped islands, or strands, which can run for miles. Cypress domes are formed as the trees grow in water pockets, with the larger trees growing where the water is deeper and trees toward the outer edges of the dome, or island, growing progressively smaller in size as the clump progresses from the center. These domes are often symmetrical in shape. Cypress trees contribute to the mysterious display of epiphytic plants in the area, which cling and grow on the cypress, using the living tree structures as support for their growth, but not hindering the tree's growth in any way.

The most widespread epiphyte in the region are the bromeliads, which contribute to the preservation of life in the region during the dry winter months. The bromeliad's leaves create

Preceding Pages: Sunset over an island of palms in the Big Cypress National Preserve.
PHOTO BY CARR CLIFTON

Left: Sawgrass and cypress strand. Sawgrass is not a real grass but a sedge, with three serrated edges and grows to heights of twelve feet.
PHOTO BY CARR CLIFTON

Right: Bromeliad and cypress. Bromeliads are not parasites and use the structure of the host tree as support only, not for nourishment.
PHOTO BY CARR CLIFTON

reservoirs of water that slowly accumulate to provide water for the plant and for a variety of other species. Frogs, salamanders, snakes, lizards, snails, and many insects use these water reserves during the harshest of winter droughts. As smaller species accumulate to reap the benefits of the bromeliads water savings plan, they in turn provide food for the birds and other animals that prey on them.

Other epiphytic plants, such as orchids, also use this environment for their growth. Ghost and butterfly orchids, seemingly suspended in air, attach themselves to the cypress trunks and branches. Often mistaken for parasites, they also use the cypress as support for their growth without causing damage to the host.

One type of epiphytic plant, the strangler fig, also found in the Big Cypress Swamp and the Everglades, begins its growth much the same as the other epiphytics, but then slowly spreads roots and trunks that overwhelm the host tree. The strangler fig eventually causes the death of its host by strangulation and continues its own growth as a single structure.

Giant cypress, often called bald cypress, are not evergreens, but are deciduous and shed their flat, flexible leaves once a year. Giant cypress nearly disappeared as a result of aggressive logging operations in the past decades. Bald cypress wood is often called "wood eternal" because of its great resistance to decay and has long been prized for use in construction of coffins, boat houses, docks, bridges, piers and even in boat production. During World War II bald cypress were used for hull construction in PT Boats because they were light-weight and would not attract magnetic mines. Building booms of the 1940's found thousands of trees cut in response to the post war's increasing need for lumber. Thousands of bald cypress, many as much as

six or seven hundred years old, were cut until today only a few of the older trees remain. It is unlikely growth periods of these lengths will occur again, although the trees are now protected in Big Cypress National Preserve.

The bald cypress has a strong and unique root system that appears as cones, or knees, surfacing from submerged roots. The trunks of taller trees reach heights of 100 to 120 feet and more, with diameters ten feet and larger. The trunks flare outward near their base and provide strong footholds in the wet, organically rich, swamp peat that has accumulated over the last 10,000 years or so.

The ecosystems of the Big Cypress Swamp are complemented by vast saw grass prairies and slash pine forests growing over a carpet of saw palmetto in areas that normally remain fairly dry. On the higher grounds, royal palms and the tropical gumbo limbo are found. In the northern half of the preserve, a few typical hardwood hammocks appear.

Traveling through the Big Cypress Swamp, and the Fakahatchee Strand State Preserve, the visitor will observe a bounty of plant, bird, and animal life. Pockets of water teem with small crayfish, turtles, marsh rabbits, whitetail deer, frogs, otters, turkeys, snakes, and alligators, in addition to dozens of insect and bird species. The Fakahatchee Strand is well known for its larger populations of black bear, squirrel fox, and Florida panthers.

Big Cypress Swamp, like the Everglades, is dependent on the wet and dry cycle of the seasons for its survival. Toward April's end, thunderstorms rich in water and lightning bring life to the area. Each year, more than 60 inches of rain falls and fills holes, sloughs, and slowly drenches the prairies before slowly flowing west toward the Gulf, or south to feed the Everglades. Since the topography of the

area slopes a mere two inches per mile, the slow evacuation of the water adds two or three months to the wet season's end and contributes moisture to feed soil, plants, birds, animals, and drinking water for humans.

The completion of the Tamiami Trail in 1928 brought easier access to the Big Cypress area and attracted entrepreneurs and workers in large numbers. Lumber operations grew in the 1930's and 1940's, and communities formed at Pinecrest, Monroe Station, and Ochopee. Hunters, fishermen, and cattle ranchers were attracted by the wide expanses of land, the abundance of wildlife, and a possibility of life far from the busy cities of the east coast.

During the 1960's, land speculation escalated and grandiose development plans for the area were unveiled. In 1968, plans to create a large jetport and a modern city just west of the Everglades, were proposed with their only purpose being for land to be dried, excavated, and used for continued development purposes. Fortunately, the dangers these plans held for the Everglades, and the Big Cypress Swamp, rallied public opinion and opposition to the project grew until it was abandoned. Congress, alerted by dangers to this fragile ecosystem, created Big Cypress National Preserve in 1974. This designation allowed for more usage of the land than a more stringent National Park Rule, but still protected the fragile ecosystems and established a buffer zone that protects Everglades National Park to the south.

Below: The interior of a typical cypress dome.
PHOTO BY GLENN VAN NIMWEGEN

Right: Cabbage palms and grasses at dawn in the Big Cypress National Preserve.
PHOTO BY CARR CLIFTON

Following Pages: Big Cypress National Preserve.
PHOTO BY CARR CLIFTON

MAMMALS

The majority of mammals present in the Everglades, with the exception of one or two species of West Indian bats, entered the region by land from the north. Most of the species present in the area are widely distributed and well known throughout the Eastern United States. More than 40 species of mammals can be found in the Everglades National Park, many of which have adapted from life in drier environments of the north to the Park's semi-aquatic habitats. It is often surprising to see land mammals such as the white-tailed deer and marsh rabbit swimming, or wading, through marshes to forage on the Everglades' aquatic plant species, acting more like aquatic mammals than land mammals.

Of all of the larger species of land mammals present in the region; white-tailed deer, black bears, and Florida panthers; the white-tailed deer is most likely to be observed by visitors to Everglades National Park and is common in the pinelands and freshwater marshes at Long Pine Key and Shark Valley. The Everglades white-tailed deer, or Virginia deer as they are often called throughout the Eastern United States, are considerably smaller than their northern counterparts, often only reaching about two-thirds of the size of their relatives in more northern regions. The deer found in the outer Florida Keys, called key deer, are even smaller than those found in the park. The deer population of the Everglades has been protected from hunters for more than forty years and the population today has reached sufficient numbers to enjoy a natural balance with its environment.

Black bears, which are found throughout the Eastern United States, are less likely to be observed in the Everglades although they have been seen near Flamingo, Shark Valley, and the Long Pine Key areas. Black bears, which are omnivorous, leave traces of their presence by eating the tip of cabbage palms, occasional raids on bee hives, and in the past were reported to dine on sea turtle eggs found along the beaches in the area.

The Florida panther, also known as the cougar, painter, catamount, mountain lion, and puma, is also present in the Everglades and the surrounding regions. The largest of all cats found in North America, measuring as much as seven feet from their noses to the tips of their tails and often weighing up to one hundred and fifty pounds, the Florida panther is an endangered species. There are thought to be less than fifty of the magnificent animals remaining in the wilds of Southern Florida and less than a dozen to be found within the confines of Everglades National Park. Solitary creatures, except when they mate, the panthers feed on deer, feral pigs, raccoons, opossum, marsh rabbits, and other medium sized prey. Currently, major efforts are underway to assure the panther's survival and increase its numbers in the Everglades National Park and throughout Florida.

A smaller member of the feline family, the bobcat, also called the wildcat, is common in the pinelands, coastal prairies, and hardwood hammocks. Active day and night, bobcats found in the Park are seemingly unconcerned by the presence of man, perhaps because of

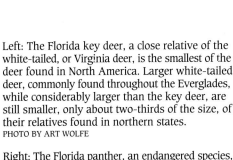

Left: The Florida key deer, a close relative of the white-tailed, or Virginia deer, is the smallest of the deer found in North America. Larger white-tailed deer, commonly found throughout the Everglades, while considerably larger than the key deer, are still smaller, only about two-thirds of the size, of their relatives found in northern states.
PHOTO BY ART WOLFE

Right: The Florida panther, an endangered species, is making its last stand in the regions of southern Florida. These magnificent creatures, after nearly being hunted to extinction, are now protected, but are still subjected to a wide variety of medical and environmental problems.
PHOTO BY ART WOLFE

the lack of active hunting by man and dog, they are relatively easy to observe. Bobcats feed on smaller prey, including birds, rabbits, and other rodents, and are well established in the Everglades National Park and surrounding regions, in a variety of habitats.

Two sub-species of raccoons can be found in most habitats of the Everglades. The most visible mammal in the region, raccoons are often seen raiding trash cans and begging for food in the region's campgrounds, a behavior most normally associated with bears in other National Parks. Omnivorous creatures, the raccoon eats almost anything including fish, crayfish, frogs, crustaceans, small mammals, and many of the various plant foods found in the region. Occasionally, these mischievious creatures, with their black eye masks making them look all the more like the robbers they can be, cause considerable damage by eating the eggs and young of birds and sea turtles.

Another omnivorous species, the opossum is common in most of the Everglades habitats and in developed areas. Opossums, like the kangaroo, are marsupials. Marsupial mammals (Metatheria) and non-marsupial mammals (Eutheria) have followed separate paths of evolution for at least 100 million years, even though there are few fundamental differences between the two groups. The feature that most distinguishes marsupials from other mammals is in their reproduction process. Marsupial young are born in a less fully developed state than other mammals and spend time after their birth inside a pouch on the mother's underside.

The river otter, reaching lengths of around four feet and weighing as much as thirty pounds, feed mainly on fish, snakes, turtles,

Above: The raccoon, common throughout most habitats of the park, is also found throughout most of the United States. Omnivorous creatures, they will feed on fruits, seeds, nuts, small rodents, frogs, fish, eggs, crustaceans, insects, and almost anything else they can find.
PHOTO BY LEONARD LEE RUE III

frogs, and the occasional baby alligator. A member of the family Mustelidae, these fur bearing mammals are the most aquatic of all mammals found in the Everglades region. Otters spend nearly all of their time in water, have webbed feet, and stiff whiskers that they use as tactile sensors. Their muscular tails provide much of the force needed by the otters to swim. Otters can occasionally be found throughout the Everglades habitats around ponds and sloughs, although they are most commonly observed near the vicinity of the Anhinga Trail or Shark Valley.

One of the less likely mammals to be seen in the Everglades, the nine-banded armadillo was first discovered by Spanish explorers who, amazed by the creatures hard, armor-like scales, named them armadillos, Spanish for "armed creature". The armored scales of the armadillo develops from their skin and is made of bony plates overlaid by horn, and are used as a defensive mechanism.

Other species of land mammals to be found in the Everglades region include the least shrew, short-tailed shrew, Eastern mole, Seminole bat, Florida yellow bat, evening bat, Brazilian free-tailed bat, Florida mastiff bat, Eastern cottontail rabbit, gray squirrel, fox squirrel, southern flying squirrel, rice rat, cotton rat, cotton mouse (an endangered species), roundtail muskrat, roof rat, Norway rat, house mouse, grey fox, red fox, domestic or feral dog, coati, Everglades mink, long tailed weasel, Eastern spotted skunk, feral pig, and domestic or feral cat.

Left: River otters, most aquatic of the park's land mammals, can be found near freshwater ponds and sloughs and eat mostly fish, snakes, frogs, turtles, and the occasional baby alligator.
PHOTO BY LEONARD LEE RUE III

Right: Gray squirrel, here eating Paurotis palm berries, is one of the park's three squirrel species.
PHOTO BY GLENN VAN NIMWEGEN

AQUATIC MAMMALS...

The Everglades, and its surrounding areas, are home to three aquatic mammal species; the Atlantic bottlenose dolphin, the short-finned pilot whale, and the West Indian manatee. The Park's bays and tidal rivers provide habitat for the bottlenose dolphins, which sometimes are erroneously called porpoises, and endangered West Indian manatees, locally common in marine and estuarine areas. Pilot whales, uncommon in the Park's marine areas, are occasionally seen off Cape Sable and the west coast.

By far the most commonly observed of these aquatic mammals is the bottlenose dolphin. Warm blooded animals closely related to whales, the bottlenose dolphin has the most familiar features of all cetaceans, with their mouths permanently fixed into smiles. The bottlenose dolphins are currently displayed in hundreds of marine facilities around the world, familiarizing millions of people with the need for protection for this highly intelligent creature and the other members of the cetacean family.

Bottlenose dolphins are considered to be primarily coastal creatures, although they are often seen in the open ocean and are widely distributed in cold temperate to tropical waters of the world's oceans. With sleek and powerfully streamlined bodies, bottlenose dolphins are natural acrobats, leaping well clear of the water's surface and gracefully diving beneath. Displaying

levels of curiosity rare in most animal species, the dolphins appear to enjoy their interactions with man and will often approach man in the wild, and have adapted well to life in captivity.

Atlantic bottlenose dolphins are frequently seen off of Cape Sable, Flamingo, and the Gulf Coast, and sometimes found well up rivers on the Gulf side of Florida. Living well over thirty years, the bottlenose dolphin enjoys a long adolescence and does not begin to breed until the females reach an age of between 9 and 10 years and the males are at least between 10 and 13 years old.

Short-finned pilot whales, which sometimes associate with bottlenose dolphin in common pursuit of prey-squid, octopus, and schooling fishes, can on occasion be sighted off Cape Sable and the west coast. The short-finned pilot whales enjoy a long life in their natural habitats, with the females reaching ages up to 62 years and the males somewhere around forty-five years. The females will reach sexual maturity at an average of nine years and will continue to be reproductive until they reach approximately thirty-seven years of age, calving on the average of every 4-5.6 years. Males reach their sexual maturity at an age of seventeen years and will remain reproductively active until their deaths.

Popular as captive exhibits in oceanariums and marine parks around the world, more than 70 short-finned pilot whales have been captured in United States waters, mainly California and Hawaii, during the last twenty years for public display. A similar amount have been captured by the Japanese for the same purposes since 1974. Unlike their more adaptive relatives, the bottlenose dolphins, more than half of the captured short-finned pilot whales die while in captivity every year. This is indeed a sad but ironic circumstance, since the short-finned pilot whale, unlike the long-finned pilot whales, were successful in escaping much of the widespread destruction brought about by the commercial whaling industry during the last century.

Perhaps the most unique of the regions aquatic mammals, the endangered West Indian manatee can be found in marine and estuarine areas and are frequently seen in Whitewater Bay, Hells Bay, and along the west coast. For additional information about this extremely unusual and very rare aquatic creature, see the sidebar on this page, "Manatee: Mermaid or Sea Cow?"

Above: Bottlenose Dolphins are the most familiar of all cetaceans, and are found in coastal waters of the park and sometimes journey far up river inlets on the park's gulf coast.
PHOTO BY JEFF FOOTT

Left and Right: An endangered species, the West Indian manatee, now numbering around 1,500 in Florida, has seen its population dwindle due to water pollution and collisions with power boats.
PHOTO BY JEFF FOOTT

MANATEE...MERMAID OR SEA COW?

When early seafarers first encountered the manatee, the first legends of mermaids began to be circulated. One must question the eyesight of these early sailors who saw the likeness of a beautiful girl in a creature as homely as the manatee. Perhaps their standards of beauty were greatly different than today's, or maybe they had simply been at sea too long.

Manatees are more accurately described by their common name, the sea cow. There are four species of sea cows, or sirenians, found in the world today. The dugong, found in coastal and island waters of the Indo-Pacific region between East Africa and Vanuatu; and three species of manatees, the West Indian and West African manatees, which occupy freshwater and marine habitats; and Amazonian manatees, which exists only in freshwater habitats of the Amazon basin. A fifth species, the Steller's sea cow, was hunted to extinction in the Bering Sea by whalers and sealers during the 18th century.

Manatees are thought to have descended from a common ancestor of the elephant and their presence has been found throughout fossil records dating to the Eocene epoch (57-37 million years ago). The manatees found in the Everglades, the West Indian manatee, is the largest mammal found within the boundaries of Everglades National Park. Mature manatees can reach lengths of more than fifteen feet and weigh as much as a ton. In spite of its massive size, the manatee is a harmless creature.

Manatees have adapted entirely to an aquatic existence, lacking external hind limbs, and use their paddle-like forelimbs and broad flat tails to aid their underwater movements as they graze on grass-like aquatic vegetation. Susceptible to cold, they can be killed by a sharp drop in water temperature and seek warm water areas.

An endangered species, Florida's manatees now number around 1,500. They were hunted extensively by the area's inhabitants for their value as a food source until recent years. Although now protected, manatees still face an almost constant threat by power boats, the major cause of their mortality. Most mature individuals have propeller scars on their backs as reminders of their collisions with boats.

REPTILES

Mention the Everglades, and most people instantly have visions of the regions many reptiles. Alligators basking in the sun on muddy banks; lurking just below a murky surface with only their eyes above water, silently surveying the surrounding area as if waiting for unwary prey to make an appearance; or hidden in the tall grass and reeds, lying in ambush for unsuspecting mammals. Water snakes, like the cottonmouths and water moccasins, slithering through the freshwater marshes and looking only to inject their poisonous venom into some poor, unsuspecting, creature. Snapping turtles, thought to be easily able to remove fingers and toes, if placed to close to their powerful jaws by a prying tourist, round out the list of reptiles ready to feast on anyone unfortunate enough to wander off the regions black-top coated surfaces.

While these images offer an exciting, if somewhat dangerous, glimpse of the reptiles found in the Everglades, they are certainly less than accurate. The American alligator, for which most visitors to the region hold a special fascination, is common in freshwater marshes and can be found throughout the interior of the Park and in the surrounding regions. During summer, as heavy run-off of water relieves the brackishness of streams and bays, the alligator can sometimes be found in the coastal areas of Florida Bay. As water levels rise, they can be seen in ditches and canals along the sides of the roads.

As water levels drop during the dry winter and spring, these saurians instinctively search for water, often using their powerful tails and broad snouts to dig holes as much as four feet deep through the mud and peat to reach moisture. As the dry winter season continues, several alligators, and many species of smaller animals, will seek refuge in the gator's hole. During the dry season, a surprising harmony develops near the gator hole. It is not unusual to find otters, herons, snakes, turtles, and numerous other species sharing the relatively small environment of the gator hole with the alligator. Instinctively conserving energy while living off their body fat, the alligators nestle into the gator holes and often ignore the intruders, which during the wetter summer season, would quickly become their prey.

During the dry winter season, gator holes become biological microcosms, teeming with the life of the Everglades, as alligators and other thirsty creatures await the life giving rains of the wet season. The gator holes play an important role in the breeding habits of the regions many species of birds. As water levels recede, fish become concentrated in gator holes and other depressions, making it easier for the adult birds to collect food for their fast growing and hungry hatchlings. As the water levels rise, these various species venture from the gator holes, resuming the life and death struggle of predator and prey.

Although the alligator receives top billing among the regions reptiles, and are symbolic of the Everglades, they are but one of more than fifty species of reptiles found in the Park, and one of two species of saurians, sharing a common ancestry with the much

Preceding Pages: Three mature alligators basking in the sun along the banks of Taylor Slough in the Everglades National Park
PHOTO BY JERRY SIEVE

Left: Young alligator, swimming through water lilies. During the wet summer season, alligators may be found almost anywhere in the park and the surrounding areas.
PHOTO BY JEFF FOOTT

Right: American Crocodile, an endangered species, are a close relative of the American alligator. The American crocodile is usually found in the north eastern portion of Florida Bay and in a handful of places in the Florida Keys.
PHOTO BY GLENN VAN NIMWEGEN

rarer, and endangered, American crocodile who occasionally can be found in mangrove swamps and creeks of Florida Bay. Similar in appearance, and size, to American alligators, the crocodile is lighter in color, olive-gray or greenish instead of the blackish color of the mature alligator, and has a narrow tapering snout that is easily distinguished from the broad shaped snout of the American alligator.

Snakes, most often recipients of poor press from uninformed sources, have 26 species present in the Park and its surrounding regions. Everglades snakes are not observed as easily as most visitors expect, in part because there are significantly fewer snakes present in the area than most people perceive and they are less active during the drier and cooler winter months when tourism is at its peak.

Of the four poisonous species found in the Everglades and the surrounding regions, the dusky pygmy rattlesnake is the most common. The pygmy rattlesnake, which seldom grows to more than two feet in length, is most commonly found in freshwater marshes. Eastern diamondback rattlesnakes can reach lengths of up to eight feet and are

considered to be one of the most dangerous snakes in the world. Eastern diamondbacks are common in the hardwood hammocks, pinelands, and coastal prairies. The Florida cottonmouth, or water moccasin, is found in freshwater marshes, ponds, sloughs, and canals. There are three other species of water

Above: The female alligator protects her young, both before her eggs hatch and after the young hatchlings are born. Alligator hatchlings, carnivorous from birth, average 9 inches in length.
PHOTO BY GLENN VAN NIMWEGEN

snakes that share the cottonmouths coloring, habitat, and size, and are often mistaken for the poisonous snake. Eastern coral snakes, with their bright red, black, and yellow rings,

are highly venomous and can be observed in hardwood hammocks and pinelands hiding under rocks, logs, and leaves. Coral snakes, rarest of the Everglades' poisonous snakes, also have two imitators that mimic their color patterns but are not poisonous; the scarlet kingsnake and the Florida scarlet snake. These "look-alike" snakes use the coloring of the poisonous snakes as a defense against their predators, who will often leave them alone after mistaking them for their more dangerous relatives. Although it is always best to exercise caution when walking through dense vegetation, the danger of snake bite is actually relatively small. Everglades National Park, which has received millions of visitors

Above: Anole, or Florida chameleon, are capable of varying their color to match their surroundings.
PHOTO BY JEFF FOOTT

since it was established in 1947, has had few reported cases of snake bite, none of which caused serious injury.

The Everglades non-poisonous species of snakes include the Florida king snake which, besides being harmless, performs a valuable service by feeding on rodents and other snakes, including the venomous species. The Eastern indigo, the largest snake found in North America, reaches lengths of eight feet and although a threatened species, can be found in all habitats of the Park. Other species of non-poisonous snakes found in the region include the Florida green water snake, brown

Left: A young eastern diamondback rattlesnake. Extremely venomous, the eastern diamondback is the largest rattler, growing up to 96 inches, and the most dangerous snake found in North America.
PHOTO BY GLENN VAN NIMWEGEN

water snake, Florida water snake, Mangrove salt marsh snake, South Florida swamp snake, Florida brown snake, Eastern garter snake, Peninsula ribbon snake, Eastern hognose snake, Eastern coachwhip, Striped crayfish snake, corn snake, the Eastern mud snake, Southern ringneck snake, Everglades racer, Everglades rat snake, yellow rat snake, and the rough green snake.

Above: Florida brown watersnakes are common in freshwater marshes and are one of three species of snakes that share the habitat, color, and size of the venomous Florida cottonmouth, or water moccasin.
PHOTO BY GLENN VAN NIMWEGEN

Above: The Florida redbelly turtle is common in freshwater areas of the Everglades. One of several terrestrial, freshwater, or marine turtles found in the Everglades and sharing environments with the alligator, they often become alligator prey.
PHOTO BY GLENN VAN NIMWEGEN

Of the Everglades' lizard species, the most common is the anole, also called the Florida chameleon, which has the ability to change its body color to blend in with it's surroundings. The green anole is commonly found in fresh water marshes, pinelands, hardwood hammocks, and around developed areas. The brown anole, native to Cuba, is an exotic species that can be found in some hardwood hammocks and pinelands and is common in developed sites. Knight anole, another species from Cuba, are rare and not known to be established in the Everglades National Park.

The Eastern glass lizard, uncommon but occasionally found in freshwater marshes, pinelands, and hardwood hammocks, and the Island glass lizard, common in freshwater marshes and pinelands, are often mistaken for snakes because of their lack of legs. Glass lizards have the ability to drop off their tails, which are longer than the rest of their bodies, as a defensive mechanism when threatened.

The Everglades are also the habitat of two species of geckos, the Indopacific gecko, an exotic species native to southern Asia, and the Florida Reef gecko, the smallest species of lizard found in North America. The region's lizard species also includes the common iguana, an exotic species native to Central and South America and the ground skink, commonly found under rocks, logs, or leaves in hardwood hammocks and pinelands.

The Everglades has sixteen species of turtles, some terrestrial, and others preferring either salt or fresh water. The most common turtle found in the Everglades is the box turtle. This terrestrial turtle can frequently be seen roadside in the Park. A favorite food of the alligator, the Florida softshell and Florida snapping turtles are freshwater species.

The sea turtles found in the Everglades rarely come ashore unless it is to lay their eggs. Some species of sea turtles will reach weights of three hundred pounds and have shells as long as three feet when mature. In years past four species of sea turtles nested on Florida beaches. Constant pressure from hunters, who harvested their eggs and often slaughtered the females while nesting on the beach, their most vulnerable stage, and the removal of habitat by land developers has greatly reduced the number of sea turtles.

Today, only the Atlantic loggerhead still commonly nests in the Park. The Atlantic hawksbill, an endangered sea turtle may still occasionally be seen around the coral reefs offshore but there are no known nesting records for the Park in recent years. Other turtles found in the region include the striped mud turtle, stinkpot, diamondback terrapin, Peninsula cooter, Florida redbelly turtle, Florida chicken turtle, gopher tortoise, Atlantic green turtle, and the Atlantic ridley.

AMPHIBIANS

Most amphibians, species adapted to live both on land and in the water, that are found in the Everglades region are difficult for the untrained eye to observe. This is primarily due to the vast expanse of their habitat, the density of the vegetation therein, and their adaptive coloring. The Park's four salamander species, all of which are aquatic, live under dense vegetation near freshwater. The two-toed amphiuma is a common, but rarely seen, nocturnal amphibian that is commonly associated with water hyacinths along the Tamiami Trail. The greater siren, a nocturnal creature, is common but rarely seen in shallow freshwater marshes and ponds and is generally associated with aquatic plants. The Everglades dwarf siren, a subspecies known to occur only in the Everglades, is common in freshwater marshes among dead vegetation. Peninsula newts are common in freshwater marshes and solution holes in hardwood hammocks.

Toads and frogs are amphibians less likely to be overlooked, partly because of their raucaus and more audible mating calls, especially during the rainy season. Three species of tree frogs, the green treefrog, Cuban treefrog, and the squirrel treefrog, can be found resting on the vegetation in freshwater marshes, hardwood hammocks, and pinelands, waiting to snag the passing insects that comprise their diet. The pig frog, or southern bull frog, can be heard night and day, throughout the year. The pig frog's legs are also frequently found on restaurant menus.

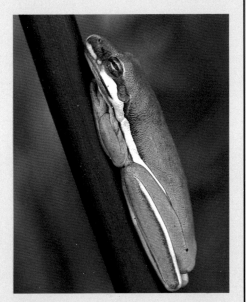

Above: Green treefrogs are widespread in the park and are often found in large groups.
PHOTO BY JEFF FOOTT

Other frogs and toads found in the Everglades include the Southern leopard frog, Eastern narrow-mouthed toad, Florida chorus frog, the Florida cricket frog, oak toad, Southern toad, greenhouse frog, Eastern spadefoot toad, and the little grass frog, the smallest frog found in North America.

ALLIGATORS AND CROCODILES...

The Everglades National Park is home to two species of saurians, American alligator and the American crocodile, two remnants of the Mesozoic era (245-65 million years ago), also frequently called the Age of Reptiles or the Age of Dinosaurs. During the Mesozoic, crocodilians, which today include alligators, crocodiles, caimans, and gharials, existed with, and even sometimes preyed on, the periods' dinosaurs. Evolution of the crocodilians, which occurred over the last 200 million years or so, has brought many very specialized changes to these successful predators during their long evolutionary history. They have occupied diverse habitats, with some species being mostly terrestrial and others that ranged throughout the world's oceans. Crocodilians have ranged in size from less than three feet to the estimated thirty-six feet of the deinosuchus, or terror crocodile, which lived in both western and eastern North America and is thought by scientists to have weighed as much as six tons.

Crocodiles and alligators are more closely related to the birds than to the lizards they superficially resemble. Both crocodilians and birds build nests out of plant materials and show similar degrees of parental care for their young. Each have elongated outer-ear canals, complete separation of heart ventricles, and muscular gizzards, along with many other anatomical similarities.

The crocodilians next closest relative among living vertebrates are the lepidosaurs, or scaly lizards, a group named for the the horny scales that cover their skins. These protective scales are composed of keratin, a substance similar to that found in human fingernails. The scaly lizard group, which includes lizard and snake species, and the crocodilians all share many superficial resemblances although they lack recent common ancestry.

Alligators and crocodiles are cold blooded creatures and have developed an array of behavioral techniques to help control their inner temperatures. Most crocodilian species are found within regions where temperature changes are kept to a minimum, although the American alligator, found in the Everglades and other areas of the southeastern United States, and the Chinese alligator are able to withstand the colder temperatures of the temperate zone. Scientific Studies show that the American Alligator, which reached lengths of 16 to 20 feet in the past but today only grows to around 13 feet at maturity, is able to withstand temperatures as low as 39.2°F, although the optimum temperatures for these large, cold-blooded, reptiles are somewhere between 89.6°F and 95°F.

Crocodilians first appeared toward the end of the Triassic period, when the earth's many continents were united in one supercontinent called Pangea. As Pangea began to break up during the Jurassic period, which happened around 200 million years ago, crocodilians were isolated from one another as the newly formed continents drifted apart and began to evolve independently along divergent lines.

Crocodilians have existed in south Florida since the Eocene period, which began nearly 60 million years ago, and were successful predators throughout the many changes the continent's environments were subjected to by natural forces. The recent arrival of man in the crocodilians habitat was almost more than the highly adaptable creatures could survive. The hunting of American crocodiles and American alligators for their skins severely reduced their populations in recent history. After these ancient species were placed under protective measures, their populations showed remarkable improvements, although American crocodiles are still considered an endangered species and American alligators are considered threatened.

Today, the greatest dangers to the continued survival of these two crocodilian species come from pollution and destruction of their habitat.

The major physical differences between the American crocodile and the American alligator is in the shape of their snouts; the American alligator's snout is broad and "U" shaped, and the American crocodile's snout is tapered to a narrow point, forming a "V" shape. The American crocodile has an olive gray-green hide while the alligator's skin is almost black.

American alligators are found throughout the southeastern United States, from the border areas of Virginia and North Carolina south to the southern reaches of Florida and west to the Rio Grande River in eastern Texas. American crocodiles are present in the United States only in the far southern reaches of Florida, mainly in the northeastern areas of Florida Bay and in the Florida Keys. American alligators are well adapted for life in all fresh water habitats, although they are occasionally found in brackish or salt water environments. American crocodiles favor a more brackish environment, although they can also be found in freshwater habitats, they are normally found within mangrove swamps and creeks near Florida Bay and around Flamingo.

In the wild, both alligators and crocodiles eat only once or twice a week and have been known to survive without feeding for periods of up to six months. American alligators, like all crocodilians, are carnivorous, and the hatchlings, juveniles, and adults will all feed on various insects, snakes, turtles, snails, fish, mammals, and birds. American crocodiles, which can reach a length of twenty feet, eat a diet very similar to the American alligator's. All crocodilians rely on the forces of gravity to move food down their gullets, first positioning the food in a comfortable position in the mouth and then moving the head backward so the food slides easily down their throat.

During mating seasons, in April and May, adult males begin to bellow loudly to attract mates and in defense of their territories. After mating, the female builds a nest of mud and rotting vegetation in which she lays her eggs. The eggs hatch in late summer or early fall with hatchlings an average of about 10 inches long. Young crocodilians grow an average of a foot a year until maturity about 10 years later.

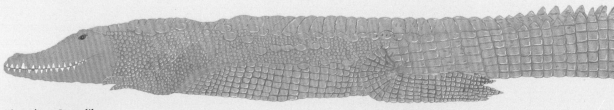

American Crocodile
Lengths: To 20 Feet

Right: An American alligator glides quietly through an Everglades pond.
PHOTO BY LEONARD LEE RUE III

BIRDS

The Everglades National Park has two species of pelicans, American white pelicans and brown pelicans. The American white pelican is second only to the California condor in terms of size of all birds that are found in North America. These huge birds, with wingspans as much as nine feet, often stand between 54 and 70 inches tall. Both American white pelicans, and brown pelicans, use their throat pouches to capture fish.

The brown pelicans use powerful dives to crash through the water's surface to capture fish, while the American white pelicans use their pouches to scoop fish while swimming or wading in shallow water. Pelicans have to empty their pouches of water before being able to move or take flight as the water filled pouch may weigh as much as the bird itself, a process that can take up to a minute.

Few places in the world can rival the variety and diversity of the more than 350 different bird species observed in the Everglades, including specimens from some of the rarest and most beautiful species found in the U.S. The birds of the Everglades, more visible than the area's reptile or mammal species, are so varied, colorful, and active, that a trip to the area can make the most casual visitor an avid bird watcher.

Many famous naturalists of the last two centuries explored South Florida, including John James Audubon, who visited the region more than 150 years ago. Audubon, the first artist to go into the field to study birds in their natural habitats, is quoted as saying, "No man living knows better than I do the habits of our birds; no man has studied them as I have done." Today, Audubon's name lives on, as generations study his paintings, and as an important source of inspiration for the National Association of Audubon Societies.

The Everglades location and environments play an important role in migratory patterns of many bird species, forming a stopping point for birds from temperate, and tropical, locations using the Florida peninsula as part of their route to seasonal destinations. The Everglades attract species using the region for seasonal habitats, and those stranded by bad weather on their way to other destinations.

Many species wintering in the Everglades are attracted by the abundance of food made available by the region's seasonal droughts. As winter's dry season descends upon the Everglades, water levels recede and the fish

and other aquatic species become concentrated in ponds and gator holes, greatly decreasing the effort needed to feed hungry hatchlings, especially for the larger species. Winter drought attracts birds not otherwise present in the region, along with larger flocks of species normally present in the area. Winter droughts also attract large numbers of bird watchers who take advantage of the large populations to observe this amazing display of life.

Although there appears to be an abundance of birds present in the Everglades region, their numbers have been drastically reduced from those found in the 1930's and prior years. The overall populations of nesting wading birds has declined by more than 90 percent since the 1930's, roseate spoonbills have lost half of their numbers since 1980, and during the last few years the wood storks have not been observed nesting in significant numbers.

Garnering the greatest amount of attention, the large water birds of the Everglades include most of the species of wading birds found in the U.S., including herons, egrets, storks, ibis, bitterns, spoonbills, and limpkins. Herons are well represented in the region, from the great blue herons, reaching nearly four feet in height, to the less common and smaller least bittern, which can be difficult to observe as it remains motionless when sensing danger.

Herons are generally recognized by their elongated bodies and necks, although some species, like the green backed heron, are more compact. Specialized in foraging for small fish, most herons feed by stalking their prey, either advancing so slowly their movements are

Preceding Pages: Double crested cormorants at sunset in Florida Bay. Double crested cormorants are found in both marine and terrestrial habitats.
PHOTO BY JOHN NETHERTON

Left: Great egrets, the second largest of the heron species, are typically seen slowly stalking prey in the shallow waters of freshwater, and saltwater, marshes, lakes, lagoons, and ponds.
PHOTO BY GLENN VAN NIMWEGEN

Right: A Little blue heron quietly stalks prey among the arched roots of a red mangrove.
PHOTO BY GLENN VAN NIMWEGEN

BIRDS CONTINUED...

barely perceptible, or remaining motionless until prey moves within striking range, their necks unfolding with lightning-fast action and their sharp beaks spearing the unwary prey.

Many species of herons have ornamental plumage on their heads and tails, which are especially well developed and spectacular during breeding season. The beautiful plumage of these birds nearly caused their extinction around the turn of the century, as hundreds of thousands were killed by feather merchants.

Fashions of the day were for women to wear hats decorated with feathers of herons, egrets, and other species, causing feather collecting to become a lucrative business for hunters with little qualms about killing birds for a handful of feathers. Compounding damages, this hunting was done when the bird's plumage achieved their most spectacular state, during mating seasons, which destroyed mature specimens and disrupted their natural breeding cycles.

Fortunately, conservation efforts were able to stop the senseless killing of these birds. The Audubon Society, other conservation groups, and concerned individuals, led efforts that resulted in protecting the birds, their nesting areas, and feeding grounds.

Members of the heron family found in the Everglades include the great blue heron, great white heron, snowy egret, great egret, reddish egret, cattle egret, green-backed heron, little blue heron, the black-crowned night-heron, tricolored heron, yellow-crowned night-heron, American bittern, and least bittern.

Of North American heron species, great blue herons are largest and most widely dispersed. Standing between 48 and 54 inches tall, with wingspans reaching seven feet, great blue herons show amazing grace both in flight and in their typical fishing postures. Easily recognizable in flight as they fold their necks onto their backs and fly with strong regular wingbeats, the great blue heron stands, almost motionless, as it waits for prey: fish, frogs, snakes, salamanders, and on occasions, baby alligators, to enter striking range. Great blue herons can be identified by their light bluish gray bodies, white heads, black crowns, and yellowish beaks.

Great white herons, considered to be an all color morph, or white phase, of great blue herons are somewhat of a peculiarity. This large all-white bird, with greenish yellow legs and yellow beak, was considered a separate species until 1973. The great white heron is found mostly in the Florida Keys and coastal areas of Florida Bay, although they also breed in Cuba and coastal Yucatan, while the great blue heron ranges across most of North America. On rare occasions, the great white herons cross-breed with great blue herons. Great white herons, not as shy as other heron species, often approach fishermen around boat docks to feed on their scraps and leftovers, much to the delight of the seasonal visitor. Great white herons, another victim of feather merchants during the early 1900's, were further decimated by the hurricane of 1935, which reduced their populations to about 150 in south Florida. A protected species, they rose to about 1,000 birds in Florida Bay by the end of the

Above and below: The roseate spoonbills feed by moving their spoon-shaped bills in long sideways arcs to collect shrimp, small fish, and the other nutrients that are found in shallow waters.
PHOTOS BY GLENN VAN NIMWEGEN

Right: The great blue heron, standing more than four feet tall and with a seven foot wingspan, is the largest and the most widespread heron species found on the North American continent.
PHOTO BY GLENN VAN NIMWEGEN

BIRDS CONTINUED...

1950's, only to lose a third of their recently regained numbers to the devastation caused by Hurricane Donna in 1960. Populations quickly reestablished, and are now considered stable.

Great egrets, one of the most common and widespread herons found in North America, can typically be seen slowly stalking prey in salt and fresh water marshes, lagoons, lakes, and ponds. The second largest of the heron species, great egrets reach heights of between 37 and 41 inches, and can be identified by their yellow bill, black legs and feet, and all white body and head in all plumages. In breeding plumage, they have long, lacy plumes on their back.

The smaller snowy egrets, also white in all plumages, have black bills, black legs, and yellow feet. During breeding season, snowy egrets have lacy plumes on their head, back, and breast. One of the most active feeders among herons, the snowy egret darts about shuffling its bright yellow feet in shallow water to frighten prey from their hiding places. Snowy egrets, endangered by hunters as their plumes became worth as much as 32 dollars an ounce at the turn of the century, were nearly exterminated. From bird populations of hundreds of thousands, the snowy egret was hunted until only hundreds remained.

The National Audubon Society fought for plumage laws and hired their own wardens to cope with this emergency. The first Audubon warden in South Florida, Guy Bradley, was shot to death by plume hunters near Cape Sable in 1905. Today, a marker stands near the place his body washed ashore that reads "Faithful unto death." Thanks to sacrifices by conservationists past and present, snowy egrets and other wading birds have made spectacular comebacks.

Little blue herons, growing to between 25 and 29 inches tall, are quite different in immature plumage than mature plumage. Immatures are white, as they begin to mature they are pied blue and white, and mature birds are slate-blue with maroon, or purple, heads and necks.

Nearly the same size as little blue heron, the tricolored heron, called "the lady of the waters" by Audubon, has a variety of fishing techniques ranging from those of an active feeder scurrying about in pursuit of prey, to the slow stalking

Left: The snowy egret was nearly exterminated at the turn of the century by plume hunters who devastated their populations for profit.
PHOTO BY GLENN VAN NIMWEGEN

Above: The endangered wood stork's range has been dramatically reduced by alterations in the natural water flow of the Everglades.
PHOTO BY JOHN NETHERTON

Right: The tangled vegetation of this island serves as a rookery for great blue herons, great egrets, snowy egrets, and pelicans, all peacefully sharing this habitat during the breeding season.
PHOTO BY JEFF FOOTT

methods of the great blue heron. Tricolored herons are distinguished by dark slate-blue bodies, white bellies and rumps, and maroon feathers at the base of their necks. Tricolored heron plumes are buff, or cinnamon colored, on their ends, and the birds have a white stripe extending from the base of the bill to the breast.

Reddish egrets, found primarily in saltwater flats and lagoons, are rarely found far from the coast. Reaching between 27 and 32 inches in height, they have a special technique for fishing called "canopy feeding." Reddish egrets spread their wings to create shadows through which they can easily spot prey, and are the only North American heron species using this technique. Reddish egret have white and dark color phases, the white phase being totally white, and the dark phase featuring a gray body with a rust colored head and neck.

Cattle egrets, the least aquatic of the heron species, are found in a variety of habitats from freshwater and saltwater marshes to pastures, fields, orchards, and developed areas. Often associating with large hoofed mammals, they feed primarily on insects and other prey that are disturbed by the mammals movements. Cattle egrets were first observed in northern regions of South America in the 1880's and arrived in Florida in the 1940's.

Cattle egrets have expanded rapidly since they were discovered breeding at Lake Okeechobee in 1953, and are the most common and widespread heron species found in South Florida today. They are easily distinguished by their short stout orange-red bills, white bodies, and yellow or greenish legs. During breeding season, mature cattle egrets are easily identified by buff colors on their crown, back, and breast, and by their coral-pink legs.

The green-backed heron, one of the smallest heron species found in the United States, is a crow-sized bird with chestnut head and sides, a black crown, blue-grey back and wings, and a white streak under the throat and underparts. The green-backed heron can easily be identified by its bright yellow legs. They are a common species that may nest alone, with colonies of their own species, or in rookeries with other members of the heron family.

The Black-crowned night-herons and yellow-crowned night-herons are most active at night, spending much of their days roosting, although the yellow-crowned night heron is more active than its black-crowned relative during the daytime.

BIRDS CONTINUED...

Black-crowned night-herons, reaching between 23-26 inches in height have short bills, necks, and legs; a black cap, red eyes, gray wings, whitish underparts, and yellow legs. Immatures are grayish-brown with light spots on their upper body and light streaks on underparts. Adult yellow-crowned night-herons have light blue-gray bodies, black heads, yellowish foreheads, white crowns, and white cheek patches. Immature are slate-brown, with lighter spots similar to black-crowned night-heron. Yellow-crowned night-heron legs are also yellow, but longer than the black-crowned night-heron's.

Also present in the Everglades is another family of medium to large wading birds, ibises and spoonbills, with five North American species, all of which can be found in the Everglades. White Ibis, a smaller all-white wading bird reaching 22 to 28 inches tall, with a strongly down curved red bill, red facial skin, and slate-colored legs that turn red during each breeding season. The glossy ibis, slightly smaller than white ibis, is a darker species that has a chestnut body with a glossy metallic purple color on its head, neck, and underparts, while its lower back, wings, and tail are greenish or brassy. White-faced Ibises are identical in appearance and behavior to glossy ibis except during spring and summer when the white-faced ibis has a band of white feathers circling its eyes and facial skin. The scarlet ibis, with its scarlet body and black wing tips, is native to South America and rarely

Above: Green-backed heron dining on a dragonfly. These crow sized herons are the smallest heron species found on the North American continent and are often difficult to observe.
PHOTO GLENN VAN NIMWEGEN

seen in Florida. Those spotted are thought to be escapees that were once imported birds.

Roseate spoonbills, reaching heights between 30 and 34 inches, are distinctive with spatulate bills, greenish heads, and white necks, upper breasts, and upper backs. Upper wing coverts and legs are red, while the remainder of their bodies are bright pink with bright orange tails. Immatures also have spatulate bills, but have white bodies with a slight tint of pink. Immatures increase the pink hues of their plumage over the first three years of their lives. Roseate spoonbills feed by moving their spoon-like bill in sideways arcs through the water, collecting shrimp, small fish, and nutrients. By 1940, roseate spoonbills

were almost extinct in Florida, with only a few breeding pairs remaining. By the 1970's they increased to more than 1,000 nesting pairs, although they have since declined to about fifty percent of their previous peak numbers. This recent decline is thought to be related to changes in the upland drainage into Florida Bay.

Greater flamingos, similar in color to roseate spoonbills, grow to heights of 50 inches, and are closely identified with Florida, although few found in the Everglades are wild, most having escaped from captivity. Rarely found in fresh water, greater flamingos forage with their thick, sharply bent, bills and heads beneath the surface. Adults are rose-pink with black wing tips, and young are paler pink with gray heads and necks.

The wood storks, an endangered species, have been on a steady decline as water management of the Everglades has changed over the last decades. Although now near extinction, several thousand pairs nested in the region as recently

as the early 1970's. Wood stork young are slow developers, nesting pairs taking five months to rear a brood, which is about twice as long as the nesting period of the large herons. Wood storks, feeding by touch rather than sight, need drying marshes with ponds and gator holes containing highly concentrated amounts of fish, to feed their young. High waters make feeding difficult for wood storks, and causes them to leave South Florida in summer. As high water levels remain into the dry season, brought about by changes in water management caused by the development and draining of wetlands outside the park, wood storks often delay their nesting

Above: Osprey feed mostly on live fish and often submerge completely to capture prey. Males will return to the nest to feed mates and hatchlings.
PHOTO BY JOHN NETHERTON

Left: Anhinga are without the waterproof feathers common to most wading birds and need to spread their wings to dry after feeding dives.
PHOTO BY LEONARD LEE RUE III

until it is too late to raise their broods before the next wet season once again raises water levels and hinders their ability to feed.

Anhingas, a close relative of cormorants and pelicans, use sharply pointed beaks to spear prey. They can be seen swimming, bodies completely

submerged, with only necks and heads visible, giving them a snake-like appearance. Growing to 36 inches in height, they are often seen perched on snags, or limbs, with wings spread open to dry. Males are black with white plumes on the upper surface of the wings and have yellow bills. Females, also black, have buff-colored heads, necks, and upper breasts.

Double-crested cormorants at times nest in colonies with anhingas, and occasionally fish the same waters, although cormorants prefer salt water areas and anhinga fresh water ponds and sloughs. Cormorants, slightly smaller than the anhinga, are excellent swimmers and divers, and capture fish by chasing them underwater.

The Everglades has two species of pelicans; American white pelicans, one of North America's largest birds, reaching heights between 54 and 70 inches with wingspreads as much as 9 feet; and smaller brown pelicans. Both species use their pouches to capture fish. The brown pelicans use powerful dives to crash through the water's surface to capture fish, while American white pelicans use their throat pouches to scoop up fish while swimming or wading in shallow water.

Magnificent frigatebirds, a strictly marine bird that stays close to shore, are known for their abilities to soar and glide. Quite agile in the air, they are extremely awkward on land or in water.

Above: The white ibis is common in all types of wetlands, searching the shallow waters for fish, crustaceans, amphibians, and insects.
PHOTO BY GLENN VAN NIMWEGEN

Right: The purple gallinules, small but strikingly beautiful birds, have long toes that enable them to walk on floating plants to actively feed.
PHOTO BY ART WOLFE

Frigatebirds often steal food from other birds or snatch prey from the water's surface, or land, without alighting. The male frigatebirds are black with red throat pouches and females black with white breasts.

Although wading birds are the most conspicuous bird species to be found in the Everglades and the surrounding regions, the area has an impressive display of other birds, such as grebes, ducks, vultures, hawks, rails, plovers, gulls, terns, sandpipers, crows, owls, wrens, woodpeckers, flycatchers, vireos, warblers, sparrows, blackbirds, and many more. Several endangered species, snail kite, Arctic peregrine falcon, red-cockaded woodpecker, Cape Sable seaside sparrow, and the Southern bald eagle, are all protected with measures being taken to insure their survival.

The snail kite, with its curved beak specialized for the extraction of snails from their shells, has increased in numbers from about 50 during the early 1950's to around 600 today by protection of nesting areas and creation of water impoundments to favor their food supply. Arctic peregrine falcon populations are thought to have been decimated during the 1960's and 1970's by the use of pesticides in their Latin American wintering grounds. The principal management activities undertaken in the Everglades is to insure the protection of their habitat and studies are being made of the remaining populations.

The Everglades National Park's population of about 50 pairs of nesting Southern bald eagles

Above: The Everglades National Park has about 50 pairs of the endangered southern bald eagles. Florida, with 300 nesting pairs, is second only to Alaska in numbers of nesting bald eagles.
PHOTO BY LEONARD LEE RUE III

is considered stable, although there is concern that unnatural fresh water flow patterns may result in a decline of fish that are their prey and could affect their populations. The red-cockaded woodpecker was extirpated from the park's slash pine forest by logging prior to the establishment of the park in 1947. The Park will reintroduce the species with birds from the neighboring Big Cypress populations when previously logged areas needed for habitat reach maturity.

The Cape Sable seaside sparrow's breeding success depends on the fire and flood cycle in marshy grass habitats. The Park is attempting to maintain habitat for the species by a program of prescribed burns and natural fires. The Cape Sable seaside sparrow may have its status upgraded, to threatened, as a result of recent population studies showing around 6,600 birds.

FLORA

The Everglades warm moist climate makes the region an ideal environment for many species of plants, including those not native to south Florida. Many species found their way into the wild regions of the park unintentionally as ornamental plants were introduced to developed areas of southern Florida's cities, and intentionally as some species were introduced for the control of swamp areas. Without natural barriers, these plants have caused considerable damage to the area's environment.

Australian pine, one of the exotic species, is a very aggressive tree that can exclude other plant species by covering the ground with stems and branches and shading other growth. Melaleuca, one of the most problematic non-native trees, is another Australian tree that moves quickly into burnt areas and replaces native species. Brazilian pepper trees also compete with native plants and are extremely hard to control. The water hyacinth, originally introduced for its beautiful flowers, has spread rapidly, disrupting the native food chains by clogging the waterways and shading bottom dwelling plants from sunlight needed for growth.

The mystery of the Everglades is further enhanced when one begins to study the wide diversity of the plant world in the region. The Everglades plant communities are so varied, and remote, that many species in the area remain to be discovered. Currently, more than 1,000 different seed bearing plants are known to exist in the Everglades, along with some 120 species of trees, and countless shrubs, vines, and more primitive species like ferns, mosses, and lichens.

In the sub-tropical climate of the Everglades, as in other more mountainous regions of the country, differences in elevations, influences of water supplies, and soil constitutions affect the environments and their abilities to support life. In regions with a greater diversity of elevations, distances of several hundreds of feet mark the differences in plant and animal life found. In the Everglades, variations of only a few inches can mark dramatic differences in the plant communities found.

The influence of the West Indies is a very important element in the composition of the Everglades flora, becoming more pronounced toward the southern tip of Florida and the closer one gets to the southern coastline. The composition and diversity of environments in the Everglades are also influenced by the unique sub-tropical climate of the region. The driest conditions occur in the winter months, between November and April, and the wettest are in summer, between May and October. The Everglades receives approximately eighty percent of its annual rainfall during the summer season, when thunderstorms and downpours bring an average of 53 inches of rainfall, and sometimes up to 100 inches in wetter years.

The influences of the warm air of the Gulf Stream blesses the Everglades with a climate favorable for growth of a wide variety of plants and, with freezing temperatures a rarity, the growth of tropical species is made possible. It is this mixture of tropical and temperate plants that makes the Everglades so unique.

The close proximity to the West Indies and the tropics, the tip of the keys is around 75 miles north of the Tropic of Cancer, have brought modifications to the way many plants in the region appear. Leaves of more tropical species are glossier and have harder textures than those that are found on the more temperate trees of the north. This is an adaptation caused by the drier winter months and the warmer temperatures.

Of fourteen species of palms native to the United States, eight grow in southern Florida with six species found within the boundaries of the Everglades National Park, not including the Cape Sable palm which is probably an introduced species. The most beautiful and stately of the palms, the royal palm, reaches heights of 100 feet and are common at Royal Palm, throughout hammocks in neighboring vicinities, and in a few places along the coast.

Saw cabbage palms, or paurotis, grow in hammocks surrounding the mangrove forests of the south Everglades and are found in dense patches with dozens of stems as much as thirty to forty feet tall. Florida thatch palm is found on the north shore of Florida Bay and has a thin trunk with circular leaves.

Left: Mangroves and sawgrass in the dry winter season. The Everglades National Park has three different types of mangroves: the red, which is most common; black, which can be identified by breathing tubes rising vertically from their roots; and white, the least common in the region.
PHOTO BY CARR CLIFTON

Right: Cypress needles extending over a swamp. Cypress are deciduous trees, not evergreens which they closely resemble, and lose their leaves once each year during the dry winter season.
PHOTO BY GLENN VAN NIMWEGEN

FLORA CONTINUED..

Saw palmetto appears in the rocky pinelands and is generally a low growing plant, although a few erected and taller specimens may be found. Silver palm also grows as a stemless plant and often mixes with the saw palmetto. Cabbage palmettos, with their large fan-shaped leaves and stout branchless trunks, are very common throughout the Everglades region.

The Everglades has three kinds of mangrove trees, red, black, and white, forming prolific and mysterious forests both protecting the Everglades and playing an important role in the life cycle and survival of the areas animal species. Black mangroves are recognizable by breathing tubes rising from their roots and by discoloration on the underside of their leaves. The white mangroves, although widespread, are less common than the other two species.

The three different varieties of mangroves, not of the same plant family but associated because of their common ability to grow in highly saline soils and areas often inundated by sea water, sometimes grow together in the forests along lower reaches of the Gulf Coast. These species do not require salt water for growth, indeed all three can be found in fresh water areas, but have each developed abilities to tolerate salt water and saline soils.

The red mangrove is probably the most recognizable of all mangroves, with its arched aerial roots growing in dense forests, and is certainly the most often pictured in the minds of people. Red mangroves have peculiar cigar shaped seeds which are extremely resistant to the elements and are partially responsible for the mangrove's easy ability to spread over wide regions.

Unlike other seeds, the red mangrove's seed begins to develop before it leaves the tree, which adds to its survival rate. This feature has helped to spread the species throughout tropical oceans and shorelines. The ability of the mangroves to establish seeds that are completely submerged in a variety of water conditions helps to create thousands of islands, and forests of mangroves, around the world and aids in stabilizing shorelines and ecosystems while also playing a most important role in gathering sediments for formation of additional land masses.

The Everglades area also contains several species of native tropical hardwoods, usually found in hammocks some of which contain more than 70 species of trees, including marlberry, mastic, redbay, coco plum, tamarind, cypress, willow, magnolia, mahogany, holly, and more. The

Above: The large plate-like leaves of the water lily provide shelter for aquatic species and help to reduce the spread of algae. Water lilies are deciduous plants that grow leaves and flowers on the surface of slow moving waters with their root systems submerged.
PHOTO BY GLENN VAN NIMWEGEN

hardwood species have long been prized for their use in traditional woodworking and cabinet work such as crabwood, mahogany, leadwood, and fiddlewood. The only one of these species present in sufficient quantities to justify any commercial exploitation was the mahogany, long valued for its superior quality and durability. Mahogany trees were formerly common on the Keys and near the south tip of Florida. They are still found throughout Everglades National Park, with large specimens observed in the southern hammocks, and are still considered quite common.

Winter season brings the majority of tourists to the Everglades, many wishing to observe the beautiful and wild displays of flowers associated with the region. Unfortunately, the dry winter season is a time when few plant species are in bloom. During this season, most area plants are in a "resting stage" that protects them from the harsh dry conditions. The most dazzling display of wildflowers occurs during late spring and the summer season.

Summer finds aquatic bladderworts spreading their yellow flowers along the deeper sloughs; marsh pinks enlivening the prairies; yellow spatterdock and blue pickerel blooming near

Left: Morning glories, short lived perennials with soft stems and heart shaped, or 3-lobed, leaves, flower with funnel-shaped deep purple to bluish purple, crimson, or reddish flowers.
PHOTO BY TOM TILL

freshwater ponds; white spider lilies and scarlet swamp milkweed flowering among the sawgrass; brilliant displays of crimson morning glory in the pinelands; and several kinds of blazing stars spreading their purple colors throughout the pinelands. The southern climate of the Everglades brings a flowering season which is considerably longer than that found in more northern regions and throughout most of the year some beautiful species can always be found blooming in the Park.

Many plants have adapted to the difficulties the Everglades region offers in growing from the ground. The wet nature of the Everglades

Above: Virginia creeper, shown here growing on a gumbo limbo tree, are deciduous woody-stemmed tendril climbers, and grow to heights of fifty feet in search of sunlight necessary for growth.
PHOTO BY GLENN VAN NIMWEGEN

swamps; inundated sawgrass prairies and cypress swamps; the saltwater and brackish milieu of mangrove forests; or impenetrable jungle-like surroundings of tropical hammocks restricting sunlight the plants must have to grow, causes some species to reach for higher levels as vines, climbers, or aerial plants.

Some of the prettiest displays of flowering vines found in the Everglades region occur in buttonwood hammocks and mangrove forests in the south of the Park, where moonflower vines, white vanilla orchids, several vining milkweeds, and rubber vines can be found. These vines and aerial plants, also called epiphytes (See sidebar this page), arrived in the region from the West Indies and from the north. Green briers, wild grapes, poison ivy, and Virginia creeper all were originally found in northern regions, while fish hook vine, or devil's claw, originated from the West Indies.

As is the case with all life in the Everglades, the most important ingredient for survival is the presence of water. The porous limestone composition of the Floridian Plateau, covered by a thickness of peat and marl, provides a surface for waters to flow through without losing much moisture to soil penetration. As the wet summer season inundates the park and replenishes the water levels, from the

Above: Water hyacinth, one of the many species of exotic plants introduced to Florida for its natural beauty, has since spread to disrupt native food chains and clogs waterways.
PHOTO BY GLENN VAN NIMWEGEN

Kissimmee River to Lake Okeechobee, which then overflows and spreads water through the Everglades, an environment is created that insures growth for these varied plant species.

AERIAL PLANTS

Some species of plants, called epiphytes, have severed all contact with the ground and grow by attaching themselves to trunks and branches of trees. These plants are not parasitic in the sense that they only use the host tree as support, and not for nutrition. In the Everglades commonly found species of epiphytic plants include orchids, spanish moss, and bromeliads, along with a variety of ferns, and liverworts that have also adapted for survival as air plants.

Bromeliad are quite common in the park and surrounding region and appear in a wide variety of sizes, colors, and shapes. They are peculiar in their ability to collect water in their leaves, and are so successful in doing so that some plants can contain several quarts of water in their leaves and base. This ability to survive droughts by conserving water attracts other creatures to the bromeliads. Insects, amphibians, snakes, and lizards often survive the dry winter months by water found in bromeliads, along with smaller mammals and birds that also use the plant's water reserves to their advantage.

South Florida has around twenty-five species of orchids, including some species showing an amazing display of colors and others having stalks bearing more than a thousand blooms. Orchids, by their uniqueness, have long attracted plant collectors and were nearly eliminated in the wild. Today, many species are extremely rare while others may have been removed from their natural environments altogether. A combination

Above: Stiff leaved bromeliads growing on cypress. Bromeliads, epiphytes, or air plants, grow on the trunks of trees, using them as a support surface and not for nutrition.
PHOTO BY GLENN VAN NIMWEGEN

of collector's harvests and incessant development in the region has eliminated many hammocks harboring the epiphytic plants.

FISHES OF THE EVERGLADES

The fishes of the Everglades National Park, numbering around three hundred different species, play an important role in continuing the food chain in the Everglades ecosystem. A large number of the region's many bird, reptile, and mammal species rely heavily on fish populations for nourishment. Early inhabitants, the Tequesta and Calusa Indians, were both dependent on fish and shellfish of the region for a large part of their diets, as is evidenced by the remains of the huge shell mounds found in conjunction with their former settlements.

Fishes found in the freshwater habitats of the park, around ninety different species,

Bonefish
Albula vulpes
Avg wt: 4-6 lbs.

found their way into the Everglades in varied ways. A large percentage were either species that were originally found in saltwater and adapted to life either exclusively in freshwater or developed an ability to move between salt and freshwater freely, or that migrated down the Florida Peninsula from the north. A small, but growing, percentage are made of non-native species that were originally imported into Florida to be used in the aquarium trade

and have escaped. Many of these species have become well distributed and are now competing with native species.

Fishes of the salt and brackish waters of the Everglades are also found in similar habitats in the West Indies and the surrounding areas. In addition to being a very important part of the food chain, they also are popular with anglers and fly fishermen from around the world as they fish for the elusive tarpon, bonefish, permit, snook, snappers, groupers, sea trout, barracuda, and the many other exciting game fishes in the waters along the Gulf Coast, Atlantic Ocean, and Florida Bay.

Bluegill
Lepomis macrochirus
To 16 inches

Tarpon fishing in Florida is undoubtedly one of the greatest experiences available in game fishing. An extremely prolific fish, tarpon will lay as many as 12 million eggs and have the rare ability to tolerate a variety of habitats and salinities, from pure freshwater to saltwater. Tarpon grow to lengths of eight feet

Tarpon
Megalops atlantica
Lengths up to 8 feet, weights up to 350 lbs.

and will reach weights of up to 350 pounds. The tarpon's growth rate is relatively slow and it takes the fish between 6-7 years to reach sexual maturity and lengths of around 4 feet.

Freshwater fishermen are attracted mostly by the large quantities of largemouth bass and bluegill present in the region. Largemouth bass are the most popular freshwater gamefish in the United States and are known for their aggressive feeding behavior, which presents an exciting

Spotted seatrout
Cynoscion nebulosus
Average lengths 16-20 in.

challenge for the serious fisherman and the amateur angler alike.

The Everglades' seasonal cycle of drought and high water levels, important to all species found in the region, is the main regulating factor for freshwater fish populations of the Everglades, and for predators preying on them including a wide variety of wading birds. From the myriads of small killifishes and the gambusias, often called mosquito fish, which have developed the ability to survive in very shallow and warm waters, to the larger bluegill, largemouth bass, and gars which often die in large quantities during the drier months, all freshwater fishes have to adapt to fluctuating water levels and changing salinities brought about by the seasonal reductions in the freshwater supply.

Largemouth bass
Micropterus salmoides
Lengths to 38 inches

During the drier winter months, concentrations of fishes found in deeper surviving ponds and sloughs are closely tied to success, or failure, of the breeding seasons for the larger wading birds. The recent irregular supply of water, sometimes higher or lower than the natural seasonal flow, brought about by unsound management of water

Gray Snapper
Lutjanus griseus
Weights to 10 lbs.

resources, has brought about dramatic declines in bird, animal and fish populations.

Right: Malachite butterfly. The Everglades provides an environment for around 100 butterfly species.
PHOTO BY GLENN VAN NIMWEGEN

INVERTEBRATES...

The Everglades is rich in invertebrates, animals without backbones, living in both land and aquatic habitats. From tiny creatures feeding on decaying vegetation in the water; to mosquitoes living in both larval stages underwater and adult stages in the air; to beautifully colored tree snails, invertebrates of the Everglades provide a neccessary step in the food chain and are essential for survival of all species in the region.

The smallest species of invertebrates take part near the base of the food chain and are in turn eaten by small fish, who are eaten by larger species of fish, birds, reptiles, mammals, and amphibians in an increasing predator prey chain that leads to the largest species. Large invertebrates such as crayfish, crabs, freshwater prawns, and shrimp, enter the food chain directly near the highest levels as they feed wading birds, snail kites, raccoons and others.

The liguus tree snails are undoubtedly the most beautiful of all land invertebrates. With more than fifty different color patterns, ranging from white to black and including bright reds, yellows, greens and stripped or variegated patterns, the liguus snails grow to lengths of two and a half inches. Most active at night and during the wet season, the snails feed on fungi growing on the sides of tropical trees. The snails are an effective feeder, using their mouths to scrape fungi so completely

from trees that they leave clearly marked trails on the trunks.

During dry season, the snails are able to protect themselves by secreting a sticky substance that allows them to attach firmly to more humid and shadowy places, as the sporadic rains of the dry season occur, they become active and seek food.

Liguus tree snails, bisexual organisms that are both sexes, reproduce in the spring and go through a rapid growth period where they acquire larger and more vibrantly colored shells.

Tree snails have suffered through the ages, almost eliminated by specimen collectors who were attracted by their beauty, lost most of their habitat to land development, and have always been prey for birds, raccoons, opossums, and rats. Currently, liguus tree snails are protected from collectors, but further loss of their habitat to land development threatens their existence.

Above: Liguus tree snail
PHOTO GLENN VAN NIMWEGEN

HISTORY

Early inhabitants of the Everglades, the Tequesta and Calusa Indians, survived for several thousand years in the Everglades region without causing damage to the environment. Studies of the shell mounds containing remnants of their civilizations show them to have been tool and pottery makers adept at hunting, fishing, and gathering. After the arrival of the first Spanish explorers in the early 1500's, disease and the encroachment of settlers decimated the local Indian tribes and set events in motion that would later threaten the ecological balance of the Everglades.

Although there is little archeological evidence to substantiate the presence of man in the Everglades prior to the arrival of the "Glades People", hunter gatherers who had grown to substantial numbers by about 4,000 years ago, the Everglades region has been argued to have been populated for the last 11,000 years. The region's rich natural environment was bountiful in providing early inhabitants with food. Remains of deer, turtles, birds, small mammals, manatees, West Indian seals, crabs, lobsters, oysters, clams, and conch have been found among the ruins of ancient villages. Glades Indians supplemented their diet with plants and fruits including coontie roots, palmetto berries, coco plums, sea grapes, and prickly pears.

These early inhabitants left a peculiar mark on the relief of the Everglades by creating the mounds of shells that became the highest points in the park. Built over centuries, the mounds are largely concentrated in the western part of the park. A mound near the Chatham River covers an area of around 40 acres and another on Chokoloskee Island had a surface area of 135 acres and reached 20 feet in height.

Archaeologists have determined that mounds served a multi-purpose role in the lives of the early inhabitants. Formation probably began involuntarily as refuse from hunting and gathering activities was piled up. Some mounds later transformed into places of burials and sacred ceremonies. It is also thought that because of their elevated heights in the flat region, they became places of shelter when at times the high tides of hurricanes threatened.

When the first Spanish explorers arrived in the early 1500's, they found both sides of the Florida Peninsula populated by tribes of fiercely independent and war-like Indians. The first Spaniards the Indians came into contact with were slavers, collecting able bodied Indians to work the gold mines of the West Indies. The Indians of the Everglades were able to resist the slavers with arrows able to pierce chain mail. Spanish explorer Ponce de Leon, credited with claiming Florida for Spain in 1513, met his end by Indians during a voyage to the Ten Thousand Islands when he was mortally wounded, while attempting a landfall.

The Spanish discerned two main groups of Indian inhabitants upon their arrival in the southern regions of the Florida Peninsula, the Tequesta and the Calusa, and estimated their populations at between 5,000 and 20,000. The Tequesta, thought to number around 800, established their range on the east coast, from Pompano Beach to Cape Sable, and on a part of the Keys. Calusa were mainly established on the western tip of Florida, from Tampa Bay to the tip of the Peninsula, and may also have ventured into the Keys. The two groups were separated by the Everglades, with both tribes extending their range to the present boundaries of the park. It is presumed they made contact in the Cape Sable area.

Tequesta were principally fishermen, taking advantage of the great varieties of fish found in their coastal environment, while the remains of Calusa shell mounds show they favored a diet based on abundant quantities of shell fish, clams, oysters, and conch found in their area.

Left: The tricolored heron was the favorite bird of naturalist James Audubon who first visited the Everglades region in the 1830's.
PHOTO BY GLENN VAN NIMWEGEN

Right: Prior to the turn of the century an estimated population of two million wading birds populated the Everglades. As women's fashions in Eastern cities started a craze for hats adorned with plumes of the wading birds, several species, including the Great Egret shown here, were nearly exterminated by feather merchants who invaded rookeries and engaged in wholesale slaughter of the magnificent birds for a handful of their feathers. Protective laws helped the bird species to rebound to levels near those of the late 1800's only to once again become threatened as over development of South Florida began to destroy much of their native habitat in the years following World War II.
PHOTO BY LEONARD LEE RUE III

HISTORY CONTINUED...

With the first Europeans came diseases of the Old World; polio, influenza, tuberculosis, the common cold and more, against which Indians had no natural immunization. By the early 1800's, the Indians were decimated, with few survivors remaining. As the settlers' hunger for land increased, more and more pressure was placed upon native inhabitants.

Indians from Georgia, the Carolinas, and Alabama were forced by the wave of settlers to leave their ancestral lands and to migrate southward, in hopes of retaining their way of life. Miccosukee, of the Creek Confederacy, were among the first to arrive in Florida. First settling in the northern regions of Florida, they were forced south into Big Cypress Swamp, and finally into the Everglades. It is thought that the Miccosukee probably destroyed, or assimilated, the last of the Glades Indians.

Following the Creek War of 1813-1814, the pressures continued to mount from increasing numbers of settlers and other members of the Creek Confederacy moved into Florida, where they became known as the Seminoles. As they established themselves in Florida, they offered refuge to runaway slaves, living together as free men in defiance to the white man's rule.

The sheltering of runaway slaves, and the existence of a Spanish territory so close to boundaries of the recently formed American nation, created political controversy that found the government at odds with the Seminoles and the Spanish. During the 1st Seminole War, between 1817-1818, General Andrew Jackson, a well known Indian hater, entered Florida and destroyed entire communities of Seminoles. In 1821, Florida was purchased from Spain for 5 million dollars and pressures for the final removal of the Seminoles continued to mount.

Jackson, after becoming president, enacted the Indian Removal Act of 1830 with intentions of moving all Indian Tribes found east of the Mississippi River to what was then designated as Indian Territory, Oklahoma and Arkansas. The trail to Oklahoma became known as the "Trail of Tears", and although many eastern tribes went peaceably to the Indian Territory, a large number of Seminoles flatly refused to be removed from their homelands and resisted all attempts for their relocation.

It took the 2nd Seminole War of 1835-1842, and the 3rd Seminole War of 1855-1858, to remove a majority of Seminoles remaining in the region. When Billy Bowlegs, a Seminole resistance leader, was captured in 1859, all but a few hundred of the remaining Seminoles were removed from the region. Those avoiding capture hid in the impenetrable environments of Big Cypress Swamp and the Everglades.

The U. S. Army pursued remaining Seminoles through Florida's interiors without success and gradually the difficulty of the pursuit, with a cost of 20 million dollars and the lives of 1,500 soldiers, led the government to allow the Seminoles to remain in the area. Today, their descendants live in small settlements and reservations in southern Florida where they have established businesses to take advantage of the tourist trade. The Seminoles continue to be extremely independent, hunting, fishing, and farming to supplement their existence.

Florida became the 27th state in 1845. Soon after, in 1861, Florida entered the Civil War. The state contributed 15,000 volunteers, along with 25,000 head of cattle, millions of pounds of fish, and countless tons of salt and pork to the Confederate States of America's cause. As the Civil War ended, Florida found itself poor

and with a small industrial base. Its only assets were swamp land, sun, and pleasant winters.

Slowly southern Florida and the Keys began to attract more people, with winter farming and tourism bringing needed development to the region. Settlements began to grow, but the isolation of southern Florida and the Keys kept rapid growth in check until the turn of the century, when entrepreneurs began seeing a future for development of the state. Hamilton Disston of Philadelphia bought four million acres in Southern Florida, becoming the largest land owner in the nation. H.B. Plant completed a rail line from Waycross, Georgia to Jacksonville, Florida in 1881, and by the turn of the century had more than 500 miles of rail into Florida, including a line to Tampa. Henry M. Flagler, of Standard Oil fame, built a railroad down the east coast to Daytona, through Palatka, and on to Miami which was completed in 1896. He added a line to Key West in 1912.

The early 1900's found Florida's governor, Napoleon Bonaparte Broward, begin to launch policies for the state's growth, at the same time advocating conservation of fish, oysters, wildlife, and forests. Broward initiated drainage laws, appointed drainage commissioners, and paved the way for future development of the state. These laws meant to slowly, but surely, dry up Florida's wetlands, a goal that seemed quite reasonable under standards of the day.

Canals were built from Lake Okeechobee to the east coast to supply water for the growing population and for winter crops of large farms. Tamiami Trail, completed in 1928, connected the east and west coasts with disastrous results for trees of Big Cypress Swamp and paved the way for the exploitation of the entire region.

Unfortunately, standards of earlier years did not take into consideration damages done to the ecosystem of the region as waterways and wetlands of the Everglades were altered. For decades the Army Corps of Engineers, pushed by public desire to extend the amount of land available for development and to control the seasonal flooding, pursued policies guaranteeing a constant flow of freshwater for the growing populations and agricultural projects.

Resulting dams, canals, and dikes moved waters from their natural flow southward, with dangerous results for flora and fauna native to the region. At first, newly reclaimed lands yielded bumper crops and there seemed to be ample supplies of water for all concerned. Unfortunately, ecological side effects gradually became apparent as reclaimed areas burned extensively during dry seasons, and top soils

Left: Extensive farming in Florida has lead to high levels of pollutants damaging the natural balance of nutrients in the Everglades. Unstable levels in water tables has turned many wells, once pumping freshwater, brackish as saltwater infiltrates water tables during periods of low freshwater levels.
PHOTO BY GLENN VAN NIMWEGEN

turned to a misty powder that simply eroded away. The accelerated erosion of Florida's top soil has been measured at more than five feet in the last 67 years by researchers at the University of Florida. This accelerated erosion from channeling and drying caused permanent damage as non renewable deposits of top soil have eroded away. Still, the cash bonanza that lead Florida to being one of the nation's richest farming areas was hard for most to resist as the state became a major agricultural producer.

This agricultural success has also contributed to the pollution of the region's water supplies. Agricultural runoff contains high levels of phosphorous and nitrogen that are generated by eroding top soils and fertilizer residues. As the enriched wastes flow into the Everglades they create a process of eutrophication, which causes an overgrowth of algae that slowly consumes available oxygen and strangles the water of other growth. In August of 1986, an explosion of algae covered nearly a quarter of Lake Okeechobee's surface. The subsequent media and political coverage created by this event has done much to enlighten the world to the fragile condition of the Everglades.

Since the intervention by Audubon Society wardens to protect the plume birds at the turn of the century, concerned groups and individuals have fought to protect the Everglades. The Everglades National Park was authorized on May 30, 1934, and established on June 20, 1947. The park was designated an International Biosphere Reserve in 1976, and World Heritage Site in 1979. Today, environmentalists, National Park Service personnel, and a concerned public are rigorously involved in correcting the past environmental damages to the Everglades.

SOUTH FLORIDA IN 1900

During the preceding century the natural flow of the Everglades has been drastically altered by development of the regions surrounding the Everglades. More than 60 percent of the wetlands present in 1900 have now vanished from South Florida. After hurricane floods of the late 1920's killed many thousands of people, the U.S. Army Corps of Engineers began projects to tame the Everglades system. They unwittingly began a process that has placed the entire system in grave danger.

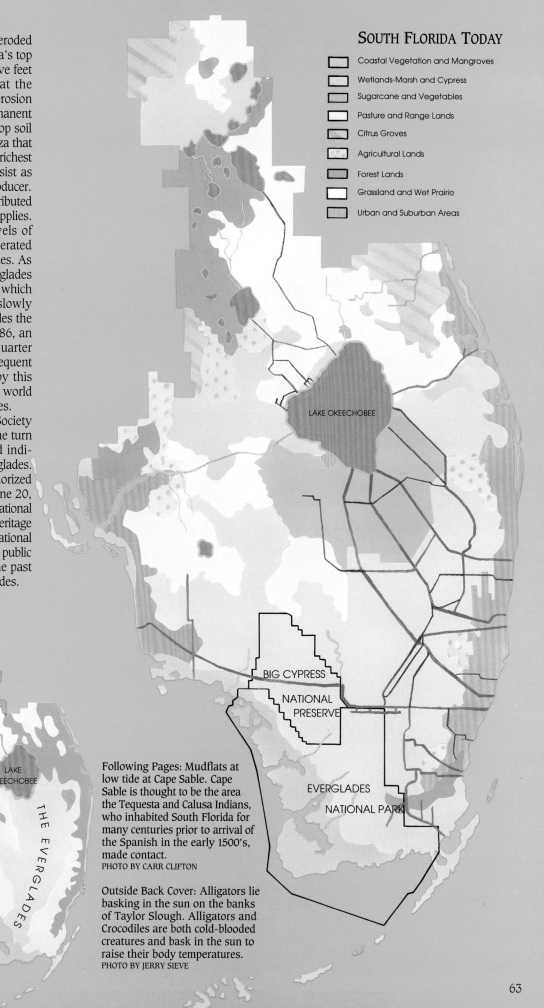

SOUTH FLORIDA TODAY

- Coastal Vegetation and Mangroves
- Wetlands-Marsh and Cypress
- Sugarcane and Vegetables
- Pasture and Range Lands
- Citrus Groves
- Agricultural Lands
- Forest Lands
- Grassland and Wet Prairie
- Urban and Suburban Areas

LAKE OKEECHOBEE

LAKE OKEECHOBEE

THE EVERGLADES

BIG CYPRESS

NATIONAL PRESERVE

EVERGLADES

NATIONAL PARK

Following Pages: Mudflats at low tide at Cape Sable. Cape Sable is thought to be the area the Tequesta and Calusa Indians, who inhabited South Florida for many centuries prior to arrival of the Spanish in the early 1500's, made contact.
PHOTO BY CARR CLIFTON

Outside Back Cover: Alligators lie basking in the sun on the banks of Taylor Slough. Alligators and Crocodiles are both cold-blooded creatures and bask in the sun to raise their body temperatures.
PHOTO BY JERRY SIEVE